GOD HAD HIS TURN

THE OLD TESTICLE

ASHLEY JANE RICHARDSON

Copyright © 2017 AJR PUB

www.austinjamesrobinson.org/pub

All rights reserved

Cover design by Christopher Sullivan

First published on June 25th, 2017

ISBN:
978-0-9992029-0-6

Some names and characteristics of people, places, and things have been changed to protect the privacy of the individuals involved.

No part of this book may be reproduced in any form or by any electronic or mechanical means, including information storage and retrieval systems, without permission in writing from the publisher.

DEDICATED TO ME

THE CHAPTERS AND WHAT PAGES THEY'RE ON SO YOU DON'T HAVE TO READ IN ORDER AND CAN SKIP AHEAD TO THE STEAMY PARTS

FOREWORD	11
PUBLISHER'S NOTE	17
THE BOOK OF GENITALS	21
THE BOOK OF EXODUSSY	40
THE BOOK OF LEVITIDICKS	51
THE BOOK OF DOODY-ANATOMY	65

THE BOOK OF JOSHUA'S BALLS	81
THE BOOK OF JUDGE ASSHAT	88
THE BOOK OF THE THREESOME BETWEEN RUTH & TWO GUYS BOTH NAMED SAMUEL	97
BIONICLES	109
PROBE	119
PSALMS	128
BRA-VERBS	138
THE DICK OF SOLOMON	150
LACTATIONS	164
AFTERWORD	179
ABOUT THE AUTHOR	181

OKAY JUST KIDDING – HERE ARE THE REAL CHAPTER TITLES

FOREWORD	xi
PUBLISHER'S NOTE	xvii
COMEDY? I HARDLY KNOW HER!	xxi
MOMENT MEMES	xl
NAUGHTY EMOJI CHAIN TEXTS AND HOW THEY'RE THE FUTURE OF MARKETING	li
TRUE CONSPIRACY THEORIES I MADE UP!	lxv

THE WHOLE REASON I WROTE THIS BOOK	lxxxi
A GROSS UNDERSTANDING OF MY SEMI-FORTUNATE CHILDHOOD LEADING UP TO WHY I'M LIKE THIS (A TIMELINE)	lxxxviii
DO YOU WANT TO HEAR ABOUT ALL OF THE TIMES I'VE BEEN A SHITTY PERSON?	xcvii
MEN IN UNIFORM, THE MUSICAL	cix
SEX!!!!!	cxix
DATING IS SIMULTANEOUSLY BOTH AN ART FORM AND NOT REAL	cxxviii
WILD COLLEGE STORIES!	cxxxviii
A CHAPTER IN WHICH I LIVE-REVIEW MANY MIXTAPES	cl
REAL ENTERTAINMENT™	clxiv

NOW THAT YOU'VE TRAVERSED MY MIND AND LIFE EXPERIENCES, DO YOU WANT MY ADVICE?	clxxv
AFTERWORD	clxxix
ABOUT THE AUTHOR	clxxxi

x

FOREWORD

Here we go… here's the start of my book! It's MINE! My asshole publisher told me I wasn't allowed to do my own foreword, but here I am! I guess he was wrong! I attempted to listen to him, but absolutely nobody else was willing to write the foreword to my book – not even the strangers at the local coffee shop that I sometimes flash my boobs to. You think they'd be more grateful. Anyway, I guess to start out, I want to thank myself for being able to write all of these words and not quit before it was completed. I would say it was a hard and life-changing process, but honestly it only took me two weeks to write. Writing really isn't that hard, even if this book is a wholesale rip-off of a Los Angeles-based artist named Naomi Elizabeth. I don't know why we care about authors so much! I mean, to be fair, my publisher did kind of have to keep forcing me to write it. I don't even know who that dude is – just some guy in Texas who knows how to publish things. Anyway, he's so annoying. Look at how pushy he was:

Anyway, once he was finally done asking me for stuff, I was able to send him this whole book that you are reading right now. And boy, is it good. I mean, I haven't really read it since I wrote it, and I'm really not sure if there's any glaring errors or subjects that will get me in trouble or sued, but I can tell you that from what I can remember, this book is good.

Now for the question everyone is asking: why? Exactly. I totally understand what you mean. Why now? Right? "How have you not written one or nine books before this one?" Well, I'm lazy. And honestly… there is no reason! Other than the fact that I don't know any publishers, I don't know how to format a document, and I really don't even know how to use a computer. Writing this book was probably the fifth time I've used a keyboard. So luckily I found Austin James Robinson through his weird brand and was able to make this dream come true.

Also, it's worth noting that I probably wrote this entire book under the influence of at least two different substances at any given time – there's really no way to be sure. Not even I, the author of this novel (if you will), can truly understand what was going on inside of my own brain while composing the words that you are about to read, and that you are reading right at this very moment. Good luck!

So here are a couple of notes I want to go over before you begin reading:

- The page numbers are roman numerals because fuck you.

- The book will possibly not make sense to you and you will be wondering why someone wrote something like this the entire time. This is a guarantee.

- I refuse to edit the book because I believe that everything I do is perfect the first time, so this probably has zero errors.

- Also, do not try to point out the errors to me because I will not be able to see them – my publisher has already tried to do this many times.

- Follow me on twitter: @GodHadHisTurn

Okay, so those are the rules you need to know before you can ride this ride. Also, just like a carnival ride, you will not be able to get off once the ride has started; which, unfortunately for you, it started the second you even thought about buying this book. Sorry! I don't make the rules! Looks like you're stuck reading this book now!

PUBLISHER'S NOTE

I want to go ahead and apologize for what you're about to read. Obviously, I'm only the publisher and not the author, but I do feel I have a responsibility to warn you about the graphic and, frankly, wildly inappropriate content you are about to be subjected to. When Ashley Jane Richardson proposed a book idea to me, I had no idea who she was. I still don't know who she is – as I have never met her and she has given me no reason to believe that she truly exists. Nonetheless, I am keeping the promise I made to myself when I started this publishing imprint (AJR PUB) and making the words and thoughts of the common people concrete – helping normal, everyday people become authors. However, I will say with confidence that Ashley is no normal, everyday person; Ashley has proven over and over again with her words and interactions to me that she a bigger-than-life concept that is the perfect combination of narcissism, bitchiness, and independence.

Throughout this book, you will traverse the world that is her thoughts, experiences, and understandings of life itself – and you *will* hate it. You will not be able to relate with her or even humbly emphasize with her, for she is a force to be reckon with and, honestly, does not want to be understood in the slightest. If anything, Ashley would very much enjoy for you to burn this book immediately after reading it and forget about any recollection you may have in regard to it. Likewise, I would suggest you follow her wishes, for I am not sure what type of karma can even unfold onto me and my loved ones due to the fact that I partook in the creation of this steaming pile of shit. Luckily, Ashley has refused to read my edits of her book MANY times, and thus will most likely not be aware of this note prior to the creation of the physical content (nor afterwards, for that matter). She has made it clear that she does not want to think or put anymore work into this than she has to, so I am able to say whatever I want, for she will not even be ordering a copy of her own book – I assure you.

With that, I beg of you to take extra

precautions before continuing on with… whatever-this-is, and to please keep an open mind, as it seems Ashley has opened up every part of her body for you. The only reason you will want to read this book in one sitting is so that you won't have to waste anymore of your time and can get it over with as soon as possible. And trust me, I understand. No one has been subjected to the torture that is this book more than I have, and I wrote a meta-novel about the weird world of ghostwriters! But, with that, I present to you: GOD HAD HIS TURN: The First Testicle by Ashley Jane Richardson.

- Austin James Robinson, Publisher

xx

COMEDY? I HARDLY KNOW HER!

I guess I should start this book / project off by stating my inspirations. Ultimately, I am inspired, stimulated, and engaged by comedians who will not admit that they are comedians. I'm sure you know what I'm talking about – hell, you probably have someone in your life like this. That kid who's funny without fail every single time he opens his mouth, and does things he deems "post-ironic" although you know he's just secretly a comedian regardless of whether or not he becomes a business consultant. After all, life is one big joke, right? Likewise, you've probably heard of RiFF RAFF, Lil B 'The BasedGod', and even Soulja Boy. I'm here to argue with definite certainty that these rappers are strictly comedians first and foremost. Although "in the closet," so to speak, in regard to comedy, there is no doubt in my mind and, soon, in the mind of the general public that these "rappers" are solely utilizing the rap game to further their comedy careers and build an audience full of people from both the rap realm and the comedy realm to maximize their outreach and influence.

Think about it: secretly satirizing a certain field of pop culture can only yield benefits on par with businesses that somehow figure out how to penetrate two demographics that are wildly isolated from each other. For example: Disney World markets itself as the happiest place on earth, as if huge crowds that require you to walk 0.0002 miles-per-hour and help you accomplish only participating in one ride over the course of your 8 hours there is true happiness. If anything, you just SWEAT half of your body weight away while waiting in line for a picture with a mouse. Therefore, they plant silly creatures all over the place to fool young children into believing that they are genuinely in a different realm that surely makes their parents' agony worth it. Disney World has penetrated two wildly different demographics: kids and individuals with the very specific kink of getting off to agony dressed up as faux-happiness. Amazing.

And that's exactly where these rappers come in. They understand that they are feeding off of the mindless fans who don't grasp how the music industry works: in a formulaic way that these rappers have mastered and are now making fun of in order to penetrate a completely different demographic – the comedic intellectuals. Now, don't be fooled, these "intellectuals" are merely on the same level of bamboozlement as the rap fans. The only difference? The intellectuals believe they are on a higher plane of understanding than the rap fans, as they believe they truly comprehend the bamboozlement of said fans while admiring the rappers for this reason. However, I would argue aggressively that these intellectuals are actually just on a higher plane of BEING bamboozled by the rappers because their vision is being clouded and, thus, not allowing them to see their own bamboozlement. The rap fans may also have this unknown cloudiness, but at least they are living in complete bliss and happiness by listening to their favorite satire rap songs by good ole Soulja Boy, whereas the comedic intellectuals are constantly allowing their faux-heightened sense of self-awareness impede on their enjoyment. It's quite a sad existence for both of these demographics, but at least it shows how brilliant these rappers can truly be.

And this is exactly how I feel about comedians who will not admit they're comedians. I mean, there's really no way to be sure whether or not these individuals are truly comedians or if they are so out-of-touch with society and their own psyche that they just *seem* like comedians. It's almost always probably the latter, but a good rule of thumb here to is to pretend that that is entirely not possible and that everyone is always a comedian if they seem like a comedian. With that, we are going to assume the following people are comedians:

- Renee Zawawi

- PookieTanner

- The Militantly-Republican Guy From New Mexico On My Facebook Friends List

Now, these people are some of the most interesting and weirdest individuals I have ever come across while surfing the World Wide Web. And, in many ways, they are the only reason I am writing these words right now and creating this book. Each one of them has played a huge part in how I conduct myself in a comedic sense and also how I go about viewing people and content online. I'm going to describe and portray each of them individually, but first I want to say: nothing is real, we all have our own realities on par with solipsism, nihilism is the President Of Our Mind, and all comedy objectively sucks. I also want to state that from this point on while we're in this chapter, it will be pretty boring and you won't laugh. This section is solely me describing exactly why this book was made, explaining why I like the type of comedy I like, and bringing general awareness to these underappreciated gems. For those of you not interested in a history lesson or the spread of awareness, please consider moving on to chapter two, where there is surely plenty of content to keep you laughing for the rest of your life. Please keep all of this in mind, and you will certainly enjoy what I have to say.

Now that I got that out of the way, I'm not afraid to discuss these individuals with you:

RENEE ZAWAWI

How I Discovered Her: So, a university friend sent me one of her music videos. Here's the link: https://www.youtube.com/watch?v=hrCIArtBsuM&t (If you're reading the physical copy of this book, just type every single character into the nearest computer meticulously. Unfortunately, you will need to click on every link I provide from this section in order to fully understand the entire book.) Anyway, that link is to one of her songs called "Happy Hour," which she has uploaded and taken down from YouTube literally dozens of times. There are still several videos on her channel that are just that music video. I honestly don't think she knows what she's doing whatsoever. But, you know, that's what I've always loved about her. You'll notice that the music video is poorly filmed, that she doesn't know what to do with her body at any given time, and that there's an unnecessary amount of grossness going on. That is, not much of anything worthy of being called content at all. But what if that IS the content? This leads me to…

Her Best Quality: Aside from being a comedian who will not admit it, I believe Renee Zawawi's (full name only) best quality is how confident she is in this content shitstorm that she's created. It's as if there's a literal hurricane going on around her and she's just smiling through it trying to convince an audience of people that nothing bad is actually happening. It's truly iconic, if nothing else. I mean, check out her IMDb: <http://www.imdb.com/name/nm2823017/> (Again, going to the links is completely mandatory.) She legitimately says, "Renee Zawawi or should we saw WOW-Y is Hollywood's new 'IT' girl." You KNOW-Y she wrote that. She had to have written that. There is literally no one else in the world that is looking at this woman and saying, "Hmm… I think this is a great start to her IMDb page. Oh wait, she's not an actress? Oh, she just makes songs and puts them up dozens of times on YouTube? Shit… she has IT!" Yet, here we are – with this content on the Internet. And I could not love it, or her, anymore than I already do. I'm not even being facetious – I sincerely love this woman and the content she has created because she has me constantly questioning whether or not I should be offended by how poorly the content has been cooked up, or amazed and inspired by how she is able to bamboozle the entire world.

Why I Think She's Lying About Her Art:
She tweets things like this:

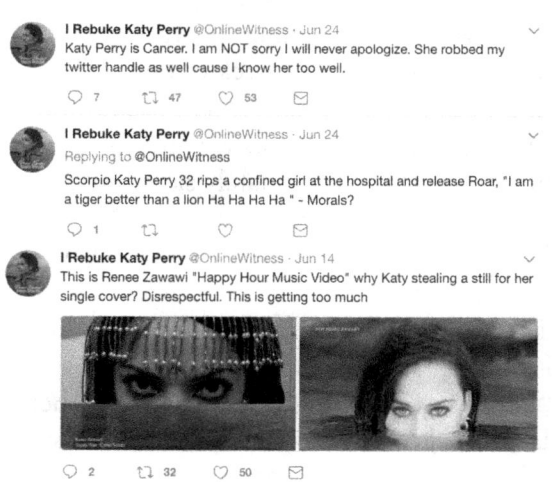

Either she has the same exact delusional mindset as Donald Trump, or she's a comedian. (And even then, how are we not sure President Trump isn't a comedian? We're not going to go there though.) Anyway, I really don't have to explain why I think she's lying, right? I'm just going to move on to the next person.

POOKIETANNER

How I Discovered Her: Now that I'm thinking about it, that same exact friend who showed me Renee Zawawi also showed me PookieTanner. I'm seriously going to have to have a talk with him. Half of me wants to thank him for exposing me to some of the best (anti)content out there, and the other half of me wants to find out why he did this to me. Anyway, here's the video of PookieTanner that he initially sent me: https://www.youtube.com/watch?v=QB0xrX8Nfm0 Notice how she cleverly titles her video so people will think that she has won a large sum of money in an unlikely way. For those of you who are too lazy to click on a link or drive all the way to the public library in order to type in all of the characters: PookieTanner is an avid candle vlogger who hoards wax and mashes her mouth to form words about said wax for up to twenty minutes weekly for her very-well-followed YouTube channel. How could I not enjoy this? I absolutely adore PookieTanner, and surely she is the only online personality I know where I would willingly treat her like a celebrity if I ever saw her in person.

Her Best Quality: PookieTanner completely takes candle vlogging to a new level. She doesn't just vlog the candle life, she lives and breathes and IS the candle life. I can't even go into a Bath & Body Works or a Yankee Candle store without thinking about her anymore. To be honest, I bought my first candle (Pink Sands!) solely because of her YouTube channel, and I get notifications about her new videos on my phone. She takes people who may be nowhere near the candle life and converts them; she's completely Mormon like that. It's so strange to me, and I can't tell whether my life has been positively or negatively changed because of her – but regardless, it has definitely been changed. Likewise, she is very good at having an overall mysterious aura about her. Upon first inspection of her, you might think she's just another teen who does candle reviews, or that she might be a white suburban college student who is just doing what she's supposed to in that sort of life. However, if you've watched as many videos of hers as I have, you quickly find out more and more facts that violently throw you into a realm where everything is upside down. Did you know she's in her thirties and is married? I don't know how she does it all.

Why I Think She's Lying About Her Art: No one loves candles THAT much. She's even worse that Ryan Murphy's hyperbolization of candle vloggers in his hit show Scream Queens. Likewise, I'm fairly certain that she does not receive any money from YouTube whatsoever; she's committing to a whole lot of work in order to make nothing in return and be confusingly bombarded by scents all day long. I'm just not buying it. However, that being said, I don't think she's fully aware that she's a comedian, either. I think she's in that weird limbo realm of sincerity, irony, and post-irony that many people don't end up in. And if she doesn't even know what she is, then how the hell can I? Regardless, I maintain that she has something else going on in that brain of hers when she's presenting yet another candle review. She might even HATE doing this, but she LOVES the fact that it's so funny and completely unnecessary and that life is entirely pointless if you truly get to the bottom of every possibility. One thing is for sure: she is hella more intelligent and hilarious than us.

THE POLITICALLY CONFUSED GUY FROM NEW MEXICO ON MY FACEBOOK FRIENDS LIST

How I Discovered Him: Honestly, how the hell does Facebook even work in the first place? I have no clue how we connected, but Facebook is telling me that we've been friends since 2014. That means that I've been exposed to him and his genius (or maybe lack there-of) for quite some time now. I want to take this moment to state that I will not reveal his name at all because I do not want to be sued, and I will definitely be marketing this book on my Facebook. With that being said, it's almost not even important that I give his name because trust me: it's a white name and everything I'm about to describe to you is the kind of shit that you would expect from a white dude who still uses Facebook in this day and age. Likewise, this means that I cannot connect his very colorful YouTube account that he is militantly passionate about and only uses to upload videos of him singing popular songs incredibly poorly on. Although, with that said, I am militantly passionate about him and would go as far as to say that he's my favorite Facebook friend. Sometimes you can't choose 'em, but that makes for the best admirations. Or whatever the saying is.

His Best Quality: The fact that he does not know where he stands on the political spectrum is probably his best quality and the most confusingly diverse thing about him. I'm not talking about someone who is moderate and sometimes endorses liberal policies and sometimes endorses conservative policies – I am talking about someone who is a socialist one day and a fascist the next. Like, wildly different ideologies that he cannot seem to decide between. Understandable? Not at all. Iconic? 100%. At the risk of exposing him against his consent, I'm only going to share a couple of

Facebook posts that he has created, just to show you how interesting he is when it comes to trying to express himself:

He literally went to a Bernie Sanders rally, spoke at it, endorsed him, AND THEN PROCEEDED TO ATTEND A DONALD TRUMP RALLY THE NEXT DAY AND DO THE EXACT SAME THING. Now, I don't know if this is some weird form of performance art, or if he has Dissociative Identity Disorder, or what. But he has so many people on Facebook confused as hell and completely bamboozled in 75 different ways. People are truly concerned. And that's what makes him one of the best content-creators I have witnessed so far. However…

Why I Think He's Lying About His Art: I have only scraped the surface when I say this guy is making everyone go wild with his posts. Aside from his Facebook content, he also has THREE separate Facebook accounts. And one fan-page. The first account is, from what I can tell, his primary account that posts about politics in a confusing manner and his YouTube video. The second one is his name but with the state acronym for New Mexico after it (NM); on this account, he simply posts facts about him being from New Mexico and nothing else. His third account is the SAME EXACT style of his second account, except the state acronym for Florida is after his name (FL) and EVERY PICTURE IS TURNED UPSIDE DOWN. Do you even want to keep imagining this or hearing about this guy? It's truly confusing and the ONLY explanation I can come up with is that he is on the same shit as Renee Zawawi and PookieTanner.

Regardless, these three people are the holy trinity when it comes to my world of comedy – and I'm not even 100% certain that they know they're comedians. It's truly been a wild experience with these individuals. So now I want to get into a subject that I believe these three people are utilizing, whether they know it or not, and pretty much consumes my style of comedy and how I execute my own content: Post-Irony.

Have you ever found yourself laughing at a poor soul who cannot sing, but genuinely believes they can to the point of putting out videos of their screeches to tunes such as "Fireworks" by Katy Perry for the whole public to see? Did you then find yourself dedicating a whole weekend or spring break solely to watching these kinds of videos, noticing you stopped laughing several days ago and are now just authentically interested in the story of this shameless person? Maybe you dedicated your entire Facebook wall to postings of these videos and some people reacted with a "ha-ha" and you got a bunch of 'likes' because you're low-key a terrible person who is socially capitalizing on the ill-fortune of people you will never meet. However, now that 'likes' and 'shares' of your ironic content (which is really just the serious, actual content of others) is dwindling, you have nowhere to turn to and people are fed up with your shit.

That is the situation I am in with all three of the individuals I just described. For simplicity, let's just use PookieTanner as an example for this section. Here's a fact: when PookieTanner puts out a new video, I immediately get a notification on my iPhone so I can ensure I don't waste anymore time on productivity and watch the latest Ninja's Candles and Melts reviews. It's really affecting my social life, but I don't care. As I stated earlier, I bought my first candle thanks to PookieTanner and I have been lighting up ever since. Surely, at this point, her death would mean more to me than any of my family members or friends. That is how much I have devoted to the candle vlogging community thanks to PookieTanner. However, it wasn't always this way. I remember a time when I had no clue white people even took videos of themselves holding structured wax and moving their mouths to formulate words that shouldn't even go together – like "it was a beautiful wooden wick, and, like, you could kind of hear it crackling when it was burning." However, now that I have been exposed to

PookieTanner, it has turned from a good ironic comedy endeavor in which I mass-texted everyone in my contact list to me not willing to admit how many hours I spend watching her videos. Surely if I were to dedicate my life to the consumption of candle vlogging content, I would lose every sane friend I have and my Facebook would become essentially void of actual content, thus rendering it socially deactivated. The momentary happiness, that is questionably elongated, I derive from this first-world content delves into the realms of irony and seriousness, fucking it up to the point that no one knows – not even me – if God predetermined me to be apart of the candle vlogging lifestyle. I am going to go out on a limb here and say, no, overall I do not actually care about which candles smell like which type of trees, but the matter of fact is: for at least the past two years, I do care. I have become what I laughed at that initial day I was sent PookieTanner's YouTube content. I have transcended from ironic, questionably stolen material for my own comedic gain on social media to fitting in with the candle vlogging community. Surely I could join numerous amounts of Facebook groups dedicated to scents and smells, and I would not stick out like a sore thumb. If anything, I am now sticking out like a sore thumb to my friends and the relationships and lifestyles I have built for myself for the past 22 years.

Therefore, either I'm trapped in an ironic prison that has masqueraded itself as comedic heaven thanks to these three individuals, or I should be put in actual prison for entertaining the fact that the content they post matter in the grand scheme of things, regardless of whether or not they're comedians.

MOMENT MEMES

So, this entire chapter is just going to be me copying and pasting content from my iPhone notes app that I've been collecting for years. Enjoy!

What exactly is a moment meme? It's basically a really dumb thing you do to other people and then immediately forget about after laughing. For example: asking someone a question and then exclaiming, "Didn't ask!" after they answer, when clearly you did ask. My notes are chock-full of these pranks and jokes that will immediately make you deplorable to everyone around you. But when you're already at rock bottom, then it's just really fun to engage in moment memes! Here is my comprehensive list of all of the moment memes me and my friends have ever created:

- After someone has told a story, say, "What?" Then after they tell it again, say, "Huh?" Then finally when they've told you the story for a third time, say, "Ohhhhh!"

- Say, "Knock, knock!" to someone. They'll naturally respond, "Who's there?" That's when you say something like, "What? It's me [your name]. Don't be stupid."

- Continuously tell your friends, "Stop sexting me!" every time they text you.

- Tell someone that a movie you've never seen is "problematic." For example, I always tell people, "Cars 2 is problematic!" This is sure to send the person immediately to Google in order to figure out what is so wrong with a movie that seems so innocent. Likewise, extra woke people will (re)watch the movie in order to make up issues, and maybe they'll post a blog!

- At performance events, scream the name of the person you're there with. For example, if you're with your friend David, scream, "GO DAVID!!!!!" even if no one on the team / performing is named David! Alternatively, you could just scream your own name.

- Call every place you go to "The Big Apple." Going to Hanover, New Hampshire? The Big Apple! Boise, Idaho? Big Apple! Literally every time I travel to another place, I say something like, "Just made it to The Big Apple – Tucson, Arizona!"

- You know how everyone always says, "Did you fall in?" after you go to the bathroom and they feel you were in there for a long time? Beat them to the punch line of their own whimsically trashy humor! Say, "Sorry – I fell in" each and every time you come back from going to the bathroom, no matter how long it was!

- So, we're all aware that the word "trans" is typically short for "transgender," right? Well, why can't it be short for the other words that begin with "trans?" For example, 'translator' or 'transfer student?' The next time you want to use any word with the root "trans," just call yourself trans! Are you a transfer student? You're trans.

- You know those people who, for some awful reason, seem to be an encyclopedia for knowledge about celebrities? And they'll say things like, "Hmm, I didn't know Martha Zingler helped with this movie!" while the credits role at the end? Just do that every time you watch a movie with someone. Find a random name on the screen when the credits appear and just repeat, "I didn't know [x] was in this movie!" They'll be impressed and not feel as special about their useless knowledge!

- Okay, so this one is classic. Take two people on your friend's list – preferably two people who do not know each other – and put them in a group chat. Change the name to something like "Anal Boat" and then leave the group. If I remember correctly, they will still be in a chat called "Anal Boat," but they won't be able to leave it because it's now a conversation between only two people.

- Just call every animal in the zoo a "puppy." That's it – I don't have anything else to add. Literally just refer to every animal as "puppy" from here on out – people will constantly try to correct you.

- The fact that the words "opinion" and "onion" are so similar is objectively hilarious! So switch them around! The next time you're stating an opinion you hold, make sure to end it with, "…but that's just my onion!" And the next time you order a hamburger, make sure to get opinions on it!

- Message your friend, "Hey I have a question." Assuming you'll have a serious question for them – maybe about them – they'll say, "Ask away!" or whatever. Then reply, "What's up?"

- Every time you throw up, immediately exclaim, "I'm pregnant!"

- Always capitalize the word "Him" – but only when you're not talking about God. This moment meme's comedy is heightened if you're not religious. And it's especially funny if you correct someone by telling them that they should have capitalized it.

- Text someone "I love you too" because it gives the illusion that they already said, "I love you" to you, even though they didn't.

- Okay this one is TERRIBLE, but it makes everyone laugh when I do it?? Anyway, you will get offended, and that's okay. Every time I see an airplane in the sky, I like to pretend I only understand two dimensions. So when the airplane is about to fly *behind* a building, I act like it's about to *hit* the building and I scream, "NO!"

- Anytime someone insults you, just pretend like you're having a hard time hearing them. After three times of you saying, "Wait, can you repeat that? I didn't hear" and them having to repeat the insult, they're likely to just get fed up with you and probably never insult you again.

- So, this isn't a moment meme so much as something I actually used to do in middle school. I would create those gross primitive chain texts (the ones that were around during flip phones), but I would put information like, "RE: RE: FWD: REDWOOD MIDDLE SCHOOL WILL BE CLOSED MONDAY, APRIL 3RD. PLEASE FORWARD THIS MESSAGE ALONG TO LET PEOPLE KNOW OF THE CLOSURE." And I'm pretty sure I actually fooled a lot of people.

- When talking about ANYONE, whether positively or negatively, stop dead in your tracks and say, "He's right behind me, isn't he?"

- Find someone really far away from you, start taking a Snapchat video where you have to zoom in really far to see them (making them completely unrecognizable), and then caption it, "Oh my gosh, I can't believe I'm near [insert celebrity name]."

- Make sure you know someone's hometown without asking them, and then ask them if they've ever been to [their hometown]. And do this a lot of times throughout your friendship with them.

- Ask someone to pick a number between 1 and 10. When they say their number, just respond, "Okay."

- When someone doesn't know about a certain thing you're talking about, just explain it by saying, "It's new." Especially when it's not, in fact, new.

- While with a group of friends, look at the moon and say, "Wow, the sun looks so weird right now."

- When someone talks about their favorite band, throw them off by saying, "Oh yeah! I love [fake song title] by them!" They'll either just agree with you so they don't seem like a fake fan, or they'll combust.

- Always ask someone about something that you secretly know about when they're discussing it. They may never find out that you already know what that thing is, but it's really fun to have that secret all to yourself.

- Ask someone, "Can you keep a secret?" When they respond, "yes" and expect a reply from you containing a secret from you, just say, "Cool."

- Anytime ANYONE tells you they're in a certain city, just reply, "I heard they have a sushi place there."

- Tell everyone that you went to UHK, and only when they ask which school that is can you say, "The University of Hard Knocks."

- If it's not going too well while in the middle of talking to a cute guy, stop mid-sentence and look at your phone and exclaim, "I gotta go! My Uber's here!" Then walk away.

- If someone doesn't laugh at a joke you made, just say, "Oh sorry – I didn't mean to bother you while you were sleeping."

- If while talking, you mess up on a word or something, just shake your head suddenly and say, "Sorry, I just had a stroke."

- Send a Snapchat photo to someone that says, "My next snap will be NSFW" and then snap them a picture of something that is completely safe for work.

- You know how people say Xmas to be more inclusive or something? Do that with all of the holidays! Xgiving! Xster!

Well, I guess that's it! Let me know if you do these to anyone, and how many friendships you destroy.

NAUGHTY EMOJI CHAIN TEXTS AND HOW THEY'RE THE FUTURE OF MARKETING

I don't know how you're reading this if you don't know what a Naughty Emoji Chain Text is. I should have made understanding this knowledge a requirement before selling this book. Nonetheless, I feel like you won't find anything in this book funny unless you know what Naughty Emoji Chain Texts are. Regardless, I guess I'll explain them in layman's terms for the sad souls who are still reading this far and might be genuinely curious.

So, we all know what text messages are, right? Okay, good. And do you know what a chain text message is? Those gross yet brilliant messages emailed to everyone telling them to forward it on to other people or they'll die or something. Side note: that's an entirely different topic that I wish I had included in this book. Anyway, what about emojis? Are you young enough to know what those are? Unfortunately I can't include any in the text of this book because every time I try, it just comes up with question marks or blank boxes. Anyway, here are pictures of my favorite emojis:

Just get an iPhone or something if you don't know what emojis are. I'm sure you know what "naughty" means, you dirty reader. I'm sure you have this book sitting right next to 50 Shades Of Grey on your bookshelf.

So put all of those things together and you more-or-less have exactly what to expect of this entire chapter: a boiling pot of everything wrong with the world. Naughty Emoji Chain Texts have been on the rise for the past couple of years, and I have created my own dedicated to holidays, school events, and even the act of babysitting. The whole point of these sorts of text messages is to be as DISGUSTING as possible while discussing a very innocent topic. I'll give an example of a holiday Naughty Emoji Chain Text that I sent out to my friends, family, and coworkers:

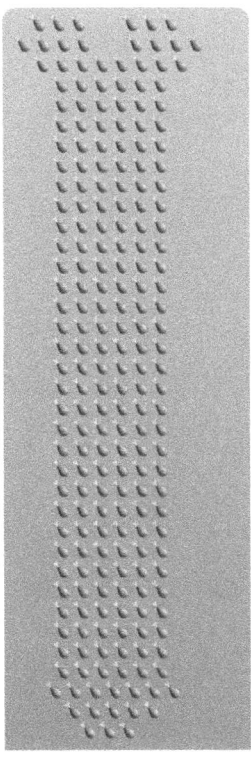

I want to take a break in the middle of the Naughty Emoji Chain Text to point out what is going on so far. I have created a huge dong entirely out of chicken leg emojis. This is almost essential. Okay, let's continue:

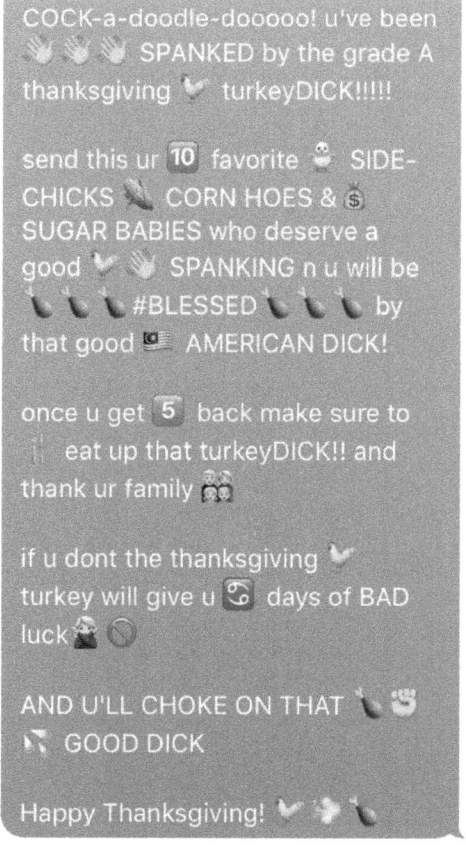

Are you turned on yet? Did the idea of Thanksgiving and how sexually scandalous it can be get you off? I sure hope so, because that was the whole point! Except… does it have to be the only point? I would like to argue that there is more to Naughty Emoji Chain Texts. There is a sort of social aspect that brings people together – bridges generations, if you will. In fact, I have seen at least hundreds of my close and personal friends enjoying these texts on the daily. They get posted on social media, sent around all willy-nilly, and created by the brave souls who aren't afraid. Of anything. These sorts of text messages hit home for many different demographics that businesses and brands are horny for. What's that? Oh, that's a great idea! Businesses can use Naughty Emoji Chain Texts as marketing techniques in order to maximize their outreach to as many demographics as possible! In fact, I would even go as far as to say that this is the only marketing strategy that businesses should be utilizing. That's why I've taken it upon myself to create one for the World Museum in Liverpool. However, I know this museum is a reputable establishment and probably doesn't want me creating peens out of turkey legs, so I made a Nice Emoji Chain Text:

✊ knock ✊
✊ knock ✊
Ashley from the World Museum in Liverpool here 👋
Do you have time 🕐 to hear about the Raphus cucullatus ❓ ❓
Otherwise known as the Dodo Bird 🐦🦃🦤

Did you know 📚📖:
- The Dodo Bird went extinct 💀🔪 around 1️⃣6️⃣9️⃣3️⃣, not even 💯 years after it was discovered 🔍🔎 in 1️⃣5️⃣9️⃣8️⃣
- The Dodo Bird was thought to be a mythical creature 🦄🌀🐚 for centuries because the camera 📷 wasn't invented during their lifetime 📅
- The Dodo Bird had its own island 🏝 named Mauritius 🏳 before Dutch explorers 📍 began hunting 🔫 them

Did any of these facts 📑☑️ make you mad 😡 ❓
Us too 👋👥
That's why the World Museum in Liverpool is here today to educate you 🎤 on the history of these beautiful animals before it is also wiped ❌ by humans 👥

Scientists 👓🔬 had a hard time agreeing which kind of bird 🕊🦜 the Dodo Bird was. It was often compared to

lvi

an ostrich, a vulture, and a pigeon 🦤 throughout the 1️⃣8️⃣th and 1️⃣9️⃣th centuries. Due to the very short keratinous section of their beak 👃 and their facial structure 😗, Dodo birds were later thought to be 💯% related to pigeons 🐦 until scientists gave up the debate and put them in their own sub-family 👨‍👩‍👧, Raphinae in the family Columbidae

So why the name Dodo ❓ ❓ The etymology of this magnificent bird is also a mystery 🕵️, as it was named the Wallowbird by the Dutch 🇳🇱 in the 1️⃣6️⃣th century while the Portuguese 🇵🇹 referred to it as a penguin 🐧 later on. However, the word "dodo" is actually thought to come from both of these cultures, from the Dutch 🇳🇱 word "Dodoor" meaning "sluggard" 🐌 and the Portuguese 🇵🇹 word "Doudo" meaning "crazy". It was ultimately the English 🇬🇧 that decided on "dodo" and the rest is history 📖, unless we forget about them forever 😱 😨 😦

By now you must be begging 🙏 for the ecology 🌲🌍🌿 of the Dodo Bird. From weight estimations ⚖️, scientists 👨‍🔬 believe the Dodo Bird lived to be around 1️⃣7️⃣ to 2️⃣1️⃣ years of age 🗻. They're also believed to have strong 🦵 leg muscles and could run fast 💨. However, since they were on an island 🏝 that rained 🌂🌧 a lot, they didn't have any trouble finding food 🍇🌰🥑 and were thus not very aggressive 😠❌ animals

But wait 🙈🚫 go back ⏪🏃, how did the Dodo Bird, a FLIGHTLESS BIRD 🐦, end up on the island of Mauritius 🏝 and possibly Réunion 🇫🇷, which are less than 1️⃣0️⃣ million years old 🗓⁉️?

In a recent 2️⃣0️⃣0️⃣2️⃣ study, it was determined that the Dodo Bird's ancestors probably settled on these islands 🛶🏠, thus making them capable of flight ✈️ at one time, but evolving into flightless creatures 🐦🚫 once these islands proved livable 🌿🏡

I know what you're saying 📣 now: "Austin, I already know 🏝 all of this about the wonderful Dodo Bird. Please get to the part about how we single-handedly ✋ caused their downfall 🔚!!"

Aside from the facts 📋 we provided earlier 📌 and the Dutch 🏝 visiting and KILLING 🔪🗡 them for almost a century, the Dodo Bird was also captured 🪤 and sent 📦 to European countries 🏴. However, the Dodo Bird was not afraid 😨 of humans 👥 and would often use its powerful 🦅 beak to defend itself 🏆. From there the rich 💰💵 held them in captivity ⛓⛓, putting them in the Emperor's Zoo 🐘🔍 in Prague 🏞 and even sending them 📦 as far as Japan as gifts

Many people 👥 wonder "they lived in a pretty dangerous area 🎬🎞️ - could that have been why they went extinct 💭 💀??" But the fact they were able to survive 💚 in a hazardous ☢️ environment with floods 🗡️ and volcanic activity 🌋 for centuries 🕐🕑🕒 shows the Dodo Bird was resilient 😎 to its ecosystem 🐾💧🌐

Furthermore, the last recorded 🦤 sighting 👀 of a wild 🦤 Dodo Bird was in Isaac Johannes Lamotius's 👨 Hunting Log 🏹📒 in 1️⃣6️⃣8️⃣8️⃣, meaning it is well believed ✏️ that the Dutch 🚢 left the island in 1️⃣7️⃣1️⃣0️⃣, shortly after the Dodo Bird's extinction 🦤 ❌💀

So what now ❓ ❓ ❓ They're just gone 💨 and we move on 🚶 🚶 ?? Not so fast 🛴❌! Thanks to modern science 🔬🧪, we have fossils 🦴 analyzed to prove ✅ the Dodo Bird existed, and artists 🎨🎬✏️ who create cultural pieces 🖼️📱 about this mis-treated animal 🦤 no longer with us ⚱️. However, it is believed that museums 🏛️, primarily in Europe 🇪🇺, have slowly destroyed 🗑️ the remains 🗑️ of the Dodo Bird, making our hand 🤚 in their destruction ⚔️ less and less believable

In 2️⃣0️⃣0️⃣5️⃣, after 💯s of years of neglect, the "International Dodo Research Project" 🍽️🦤🏹 was

lix

created to explore 🔍 the Mare aux Songes swamp in Mauritius 🇲🇺 for remains of our late friends 🦴☠️☹️. They found the fossils 🦴 of 1️⃣7️⃣ Dodo Birds, dating them back ⬅️📅 to 4️⃣2️⃣0️⃣0️⃣ years ago. The various bones 💀 found in this swamp have supplied 🔎 2️⃣6️⃣ museums 🏛️ around the world 🌍🌎🌏 (including us!), making sure they're in our memories forever 👻👻

Remember 😊 Alice's Adventures in Wonderland 👧🐇? This book 📕 by Lewis Carroll 👨‍🦰🖋️ was the first major piece of art 🎨 created featuring the Dodo Bird, making its popularity 📈 exponentially increase 📈 as a cultural icon 🏅 of extinction ⚔️. This largely led to the islands 🏝️ of Mauritius 🇲🇺 and Réunion 🇫🇷 using the Dodo Bird as their mascot 🏃, being included on their money 💵 and coat of arms 🛡️. Species of endangered 😢 animals found in current day 📅 are often named after the Dodo Bird, such as Nephilengys dodo and Pseudolasius dodo, to showcase the importance ✅ of species preservation 🆘 and keep the Dodo Bird's name alive 💾

Now if you 😊👵👴 want to spread the word 🎙️ about the Dodo Bird 🐦 and keep them in our hearts ❤️, send this to 5️⃣ people 👥 in the next 1️⃣0️⃣ minutes

Tell them the World Museum in Liverpool sent you 😢

CITATIONS:

1 - http://julianhume.co.uk/wp-content/uploads/2010/07/Hume-et-al-Owen-and-dodo.pdf
2 - https://archive.org/details/dodoitskindredor00stri
3 - http://linkinghub.elsevier.com/retrieve/pii/S0753396905000170
4 - https://www.jstor.org/stable/40983723?seq=1#page_scan_tab_contents
5 - http://www.journals.uchicago.edu/doi/10.1086/316701
6 - http://www.tandfonline.com/doi/full/10.1080/02724634.2015.1121723
7 - https://books.google.ca/books?id=bp8wk8zCg7wC&pg=PA178&redir_esc=y#v=onepage&q&f=false
8 - http://julianhume.co.uk/wp-content/uploads/2010/07/History-of-the-dodo-Hume.pdf
9 - https://books.google.ca/books?vid=9780007145720&redir_esc=y
10 - http://onlinelibrary.wiley.com/doi/10.1111/j.1469-7998.1993.tb02686.x/abstract
11 - https://www.newscientist.com/article/mg13918684.300-justice-at-last-for-the-dodo/
12 - http://www.tandfonline.com/doi/full/10.1080/02724634.2015.1113803
13 - http://m.ihc.oxfordjournals.org/content/13/2/125

So there you have it. The World Museum of Liverpool could easily hire me as their Marketing Director after viewing the art I just created. Now, my hope is that every business starts utilizing the art and popularity of Naughty Emoji Chain Texts. Will they? No – sometimes businesses just aren't that smart. In the meantime, create some Naughty Emoji Chain Texts and send them to your local businesses and senators! Then send them over to me. You could even make them about, like,… semiconductors! Or literally anything else. Maybe about the 2000 presidential election and how Al Gore deserves a lot more of our appreciation. Those are just ideas for you to get the creative juices flowing.

However, all of this good coming out of these sorts of text messages has me thinking… can we make education funny? The answer is no. Because education and information are already the funniest things to exist. Don't believe me? Just try reading a textbook about aerospace engineering for a couple of hours. That shit is funny as fuck. The key is in the mindset – you have to BELIEVE that what you're reading is hilarious. Otherwise, you become enslaved to the same thinking as the rest of your classmates who think education is boring and Harry Potter is cool. No thanks. The absolute funniest thing I have ever engaged in was the reading of my tenth grade World History textbook and cry-laughing on the page about the Industrial Revolution. Of course I understand that it's not *inherently* funny to the common person's brain – that's why you have to use your imagination! I don't even have any tangible or realistic tricks for you to try while learning in order to achieve this level of heightened humor – I just suggest that you simply *believe* the information is funny and then start laughing. It's truly the best way to comprehend and remember the information your teachers and professors are throwing at you.

In fact, I'd like to disprove that the current education system works. Likewise, I'd like to wage a formal protest against those who are suggesting we shift over to Common Core in order to teach the children of our great nation. We know exactly what they need – memes. And what's a better meme that education? Instead of presenting education and information as things they *need to learn*, how about presenting them as things they *are so very fortunate to be able to laugh at*. If teachers were comedians and came into class the first day, microphone in hand, and said something like, "So I was at the library the other day…" THEN ALL OF THE STUDENTS WOULD HAVE A LOT HIGHER TEST SCORES. Anyway, I've failed every class I've ever taken.

TRUE CONSPIRACY THEORIES I MADE UP!

This chapter is literally just going to be conspiracy theories made up on the spot by me FOR YOU. Okay, so before I get started, I do want to say that there is a blatantly obvious formula when it comes to creating conspiracy theories. Obviously, you want to make the theory sound ridiculous, but not too ridiculous to the point where the general public knows it's a lie. Remember: you want to borderline mentally separate the "intellectuals" from the people who will be willing to believe you to the point of making it the entire core of their being and tweet about it non-stop. That's why you need to take a widespread property in pop culture –

maybe a celebrity everyone mindlessly loves – and form the conspiracy theory *around* it.

Let's take Taylor Swift, for example. So, we're going to start creating a bunch of fake facts around the person that is Taylor Swift. First, we need to think of something that is completely out-of-the-blue for Taylor to be associated with. What's an event or a point-of-view that Taylor would never be caught near? OH, THE 1989 AFGHAN CIVIL WAR! It's perfect. It takes two things that are hard to believe Taylor would ever be connected to: Afghanistan and WAR. Plus, it's pretty ridiculous, so that brings out those "intellectuals" who will complain about how clearly fake this conspiracy theory is.

It's important to note that the whole point of a conspiracy theory is to make sure that as many people see it as possible, regardless of whether they're complaining about it or believing in it. That's why we need these "intellectuals" – they are the negative target market. Of course, the positive target market is the Brazilians. After the "2002 death and replacement of Avril Lavigne" they will believe literally anything.

Anyway, back to the theory. Okay, so the key point that connects Afghanistan and War to Taylor Swift is the fact that they both absolutely love the year 1989. This is what is called the *connection*. It's something that is placed deep within the two variables (in this instance, Taylor and the Afghan Civil War), but is not obvious to just anybody. It's truly excavated by only the most woke minds (or completely made up).

So now that we have our *variables* and our *connection,* we need to figure out the *claim.* The claim is what we are trying we state about Taylor Swift and the Afghan Civil War – it's the whole energy of the conspiracy theory; the tagline, if you will. Because war typically has soldiers, let's make the claim be: TAYLOR SWIFT SERVED IN THE 1989 AFGHAN CIVIL WAR BEFORE ESCAPING TO THE UNITED STATES TO BECOME A MUSIC STAR. Now, of course, this is a bit long to be an eye-catching conspiracy theory tagline / title. People are going to read that and immediately fall asleep after the fifth word – it's just how we were engineered. That's why it's important to shorten your conspiracy theory claim to as short as possible. It's all marketing, really. Let's try: TAYLOR SWIFT 1989 AFGHANISTAN SOLDIER? Perfect. Now we have the perfect claim that will blow up on social media, wreak havoc on both the "intellectuals" and the lives of those who will drop everything to believe this, and add to the already extensive and ridiculous conspiracy theory market.

But exactly how are we going to make people believe that Taylor Swift was a soldier in the 1989 Afghan Civil War? There's clearly not enough evidence from what we've already dug up. The year 1989 just simply isn't enough to convince people or make them mad enough. I know, calm the fuck down; we're getting there. Allow me to introduce the *factors*. The factors are a list of things that could back up the connection being made between the two variables and, thus, improve the reliability of the claim. For example, digging into the past of Taylor Swift and finding anything that could be connected to war, Afghanistan, spontaneously becoming a music star, or serving as a soldier is where we start. Now, luckily Taylor Swift named an entire album after the year 1989. Therefore, we're only going to be burrowing into this one album in order to make up all the factors we're going to need to complete this conspiracy theory. You don't want to focus on *too many* aspects of the variables because the followers will have very underdeveloped brains and they will not be able to process that much. Sorry about that.

While cruising the Taylor Swift 1989 Album Wikipedia page, I immediately noticed that almost half of the songs from the album were made into singles. This is a good starting point – the songs that are more prominently displayed to the public are not only going to be more well-known, but they're also going to be easier to mask as *factors* because you just have to say "why else would Taylor Swift pour so much importance into this song" or some bullshit and, idk, it just carries more weight that way. Anyway, let's just use those songs to sort of create a wall of pinpoints and strings that connect everything together. No matter how dumb you make this, honestly it's probably going to work.

Okay, so let's review. The formula for a successful conspiracy theory is below:

$$claim = \frac{(variable + variable) \times connection}{factors}$$

Don't worry if it makes literally zero sense right now. The only thing important is that we're creating a conspiracy theory to simultaneously piss off and bamboozle the world – very similar to art, in general. But to put the formula into words: First you need to have multiple *variables* that you can put into a pool that can all start to string together via a *connection*. This is how you're going to be able to come up with your *claim*, which is essentially what everyone is going to initially see of your conspiracy theory. Then all of that is going to depend on the several *factors* you'll utilize in order to give legitimacy to the entirety of the conspiracy theory. Its success depends on how all of these flow together and the likelihood that you're going to convince AND anger different types of people, already discussed.

Anyway, I think we're finally ready to unveil our new conspiracy theory to the world:

TAYLOR SWIFT SERVED IN THE 1989 AFGHAN CIVIL WAR

Trust me; our most beloved country-turned-pop artist served in the Afghan Civil War in the year 1989. Think about it – really think about it. T.

Swift's latest album, entitled 1989, provides us with bop after bop and tons of lyrics and song titles that specifically discuss her time in the 1989 Afghan Civil War. Aside from releasing her hit single "Blank Space" literally the day before Veterans Day, Swift has even used her album's title as a way to reference the year in which she served. This is an album of someone who is trying to reach out to her fans and the public in order to showcase the difficulties she went through all those years ago. Let's take a look at the singles from the album:

1. **Shake It Off**
   The first single from the album was released 2.5 months before the album release, possibly signaling the theme for the entire track list: her having to shake off the memories of fighting in an unjust war.

2. **Blank Space**
   The second single, again released the day before Veterans Day, is about her keeping track of all of the men she has murdered in the result of the war. She sings to the opposing warriors, alerting them of possible torture and flames, while taking names on her blank space.

3. ***Style***
   We're gonna skip this one. It's too deep and triggering to bring up.

4. ***Bad Blood***
   The fourth single is the most obvious of her tracks, discussing the blood shed by thousands of her victims and how she had to make enemies in order to continue. It made for a great song and music video tho.

5. ***Wildest Dream***
   Because these are going in chronological order, the fifth single is when Swift begins to dream of freedom and forgiveness. Although they seem "wild," her dreams of "burning it down" and starting a new life (possibly in the US?) resonate with us until we remember that she was in a war and we were not.

6. ***Out Of The Woods***
   Swift's sixth single sparks the beginning of her end of service, where she literally whispers, "Are we out of the woods yet?" over and over again, symbolizing her want of the war to be over. She can be heard throughout the song reminiscing on old war

times, but ultimately wanting to escape the war and start fresh.

7. **New Romantics**
   "We're all bored / We're all so tired of everything / We wait for / Trains that just aren't coming" begins her seventh single, and continues on to clearly discuss the end of the war, but the beginning of her doubt that it's all going to be OK. This final single perfectly signifies her final call for help in the 1989 Afghan Civil War.

And there you have it: definite PROOF that a major music star served in a war in Afghanistan. I still can't believe it. Please share with your family so that everyone becomes aware of what no one seems to be talking about: T. Swift being a veteran. You do love your family, don't you? YouTube video coming soon.

Now I'm going to conclude our lesson here by presenting you with a few extra points to help you create that wildly successful conspiracy theory.

First: You're going to want to repeat the *claim* over and over again, even to the point where it becomes incredibly annoying. For some reason, repeating the claim actually makes people *believe* you more – it's weird, but whatever. Notice how I said, "Taylor Swift served in the 1989 Afghan Civil War" probably about 1,989 times? And I don't even think that was enough. Don't be afraid to make the entire article your claim written over and over again.

Second: You need to talk with COMPLETE confidence. The more confidence you exude, the more annoyed "intellectuals" are going to get and the more confident Brazilians are going to be in believing your conspiracy theory and telling their family members. Plus, who doesn't love a good, confident person? Never admit that you're wrong.

Third: Create a list for the factors, such as I did with all seven singles, so that people don't get bored and force-quit your content. The common person does not know how to read an article unless it is in a list format – that's why Buzzfeed was created. Not to mention, the average person actually does not know how to read, but we're going to get to that in the next piece of advice…

Fourth: …Create a YouTube video! All of the good conspiracy theories have a YouTube video in addition to a blog. If you don't have a really poorly created YouTube video that was made in Windows MovieMaker, then absolutely no one is going to believe your claim, not even the Brazilians. What a waste of your hard work and energy at that point. Smh.

Fifth: If a *factor* doesn't make sense, don't dwell on it! In fact, just create a distraction. Notice how I didn't even give proper evidence to the third single: *Style*? I got away with that because I pretended to avoid a problematic explanation. This works great in the social justice community, and it bamboozles them every time! Thank God for trigger warnings and avoiding healthy personal growth!

Sixth: Tell people they don't love their grandparents if they don't believe in your conspiracy theory.

Now I'm going to give you one more example of a conspiracy theory so that you may get started on your own. I'm not going to go into the details of this one; I'm strictly going to tell it to you so that you have more models. In this conspiracy theory, I'm going to utilize images and scientists in order to "prove" my *factors* and *claim*. Remember to be on the look out for all of the parts of the formula and for the extra points I outlined in the previous section.

FIVE TIMES SCIENTISTS PROVED THAT FLORIDA IS NOT REAL

Some of you may be reading this title and thinking to yourself, "What is Florida?" Exactly. Florida is a "state" in the United States of America that "looks" like this:

Goofy, right? Not only that, but when Florida was supposedly added as a state on March 3rd, 1498, no one was there to witness Benjamin Franklin sign the documents. In fact, it's a little known fact that there's a fact out there stating Florida was actually and factually titled "Florkah" on these documents.

But enough of what you most likely already know about this imaginary land. To be frank and factual, there is no Florida. And here are five times SCIENTISTS proved that:

1. **All of the Cars from "Florida" are everywhere except ... Florida!**
   For those of us paying attention to license plates, we see cars zooming around all over the place no matter where we go that say "FLORIDA" on the back. A study conducted by real and living scientists who have degrees from universities and applied and interviewed for their job observed that 80% of cars seen at any given place – excluding the state where these cars are being noticed – are from Florida. So, what exactly are these cars doing away from their home "state" of Florida? And if there are no cars in Florida, then how exactly is it real?

2. **"Disney World" – like the Moon Landing – is a capitalistic green screen scheme that utilizes and abuses your closest friendships and turns everyone against you.**
   I know, I know what you're thinking: "But what about Disney World!?" What? You still believe in that?? If you still believe in Santa Clause or the Tooth Fairy or Andrew The Candy Dog, THEN IMMEDIATELY QUIT READING. We're trying to provide factual information here, not break hearts. Remember the "Moon Landing?" Green screen technology has really advanced, and your friends who claim they go to the "Happiest Place On Earth" every summer may just be lying to you. You can thank the Koch Brothers, Enron, and Fracking for this capitalistic lie tearing friendships apart every day.

3. **Many politicians and political controversies are bred from Florida, which is convenient considering IT'S NOT REAL.**
   You think Florida actually caused Al Gore to lose the 2000 presidential election against George Bush? Yeah right. I guess you also believe that Kanye West deserved that 2008

Grammy Award for Good Life instead of Soulja Boy's Crank Dat. Give me a break! Come on! Don't be silly! Pass me the rock! And you think Florida can casually have TWO candidates in the 2016 presidential election? Psh, cut me some slack. Of course political machines are going to utilize a fake land to breed lies for the people of this nation to believe in order to continue thinking the government isn't trying to just harbor our breadsticks from good ole Olive Garden – but that's a whole different argument.

4. **My parents told me I was born in Florida, but I don't remember it.**
   Coincidence? Probably.

5. **Your grandma, Judy.**
   Have you ever really met your grandma, Judy, before? Neither have I. So, where is she? Have you checked your attic? Your parents aren't going to tell you the truth. You've already discovered by now that your friends, family, and everyone you've ever known are lying to you about the reality of Florida. Run away. Get out of the country before you start believing it, too. It's too late for your grandma, Judy, but maybe not for you.

Now before you try to call this factual information out as a "conspiracy theory" and liken it to "The earth is flat!" I want to remind you that you have actually never been to Florida. Kind of easy to create a fake state when no one actually cares enough to go. Checkmate.

In conclusion, Florida is not real. I know the government may be after me for this one, but it's about time people wake up! and start realizing that not everything your United States Geography teacher taught you in high school is correct.

There you go. Two conspiracy theories created specifically for you – to help you go out and create your own conspiracy theories to annoy and bamboozle the world with.

THE WHOLE REASON I WROTE THIS BOOK

Okay, so I've already discussed exactly which "comedians" influence me and why I do what I do and think how I think. That's all in chapter one. However, I left out one very specific person that is literally the reason I'm even going through with this book: Naomi Elizabeth. Now, she is actually an artist and utilizes comedy to portray her art and host a platform. However, she could *very easily* be considered a candidate for a person who will not admit that they are ultimately a comedian. That being said though, her content is more cohesive than the rest of the individuals I mentioned… and after you view her stuff, you'll wonder exactly how the fuck that is possible.

Now, I don't want to spend too much time discussing Naomi because she will probably hate everything about this, and honestly I don't deserve to be able to say her name. Basically she makes music and videos and content for the Internet. Here's a couple of links to her music and videos for you to enjoy:

God Sent Me Here To Rock You:
https://www.youtube.com/watch?v=epRMpS5lk2I

Smooth Like Power Steering:
https://www.youtube.com/watch?v=zY3VBQGPrvo

The Topic Is Ass:
https://www.youtube.com/watch?v=VqOgzdEmkJk

As for her god-tier content for the Internet, here's a couple of the "memes" she has created for her Facebook, Tumblr, Twitter, and all other social media:

So, as you can tell, she is smarter and funnier than all of us. So much that even Grimes is enamored by her. That's right – famous musician, Canadian, and renegade badass Grimes actually keeps up with the content of Naomi Elizabeth. Which means that we are all legally required to do the same. In fact, Grimes is how I discovered Naomi Elizabeth, because Grimes reposted this song on her SoundCloud:
https://soundcloud.com/naomielizabet/carmen-choeur-des-gamins

From there, I decided that I would become obsessed with Naomi Elizabeth to the point of purchasing every single piece of content she's ever produced and promptly getting everyone in my life also involved with my obsession (which ruined several relationships, understandably). If you want to know the most direct way that she inspired me to create this book, check out the first chapter of the first (of three) book she wrote below:

I Am A Hologram From 2046

By Naomi Elizabeth

My, uh, innermost thoughts, apparently

https://soundcloud.com/naomielizabet/i-am-a-hologram-from-2046

Apparently both of her SoundCloud links are not working when I click on them, but I promise they are real – just copy and paste them into your search engine. All of her audiobooks are on Spotify and available on her website, which I will include later. Please support her or stop reading this book immediately. Oh, and by later I actually meant right now:

http://naomielizabeth.com/

All right! I guess that's it! Bye!

A GROSS UNDERSTANDING OF MY SEMI-FORTUNATE CHILDHOOD LEADING UP TO WHY I'M LIKE THIS (A TIMELINE)

This book wouldn't be complete if I didn't include a collection of micro-stories telling scattered tales throughout my childhood. All of these stories more-or-less helped form who I am as a person and led me on the unfortunate path to writing this book. So, you can thank the people within these stories (and throughout the book) for giving me the false sense of self-importance that became a pre-requisite for me to write these words right now. Anyway, they are in chronological order and if you have any kids that are these ages (or if you are one of these ages), maybe think about what experiences are helping fuck you up as a human being.

Age 5 to 10: My grandparents rescued a kid on the side of the road in the countryside. By kid, I mean a baby goat. Although, this goat was basically like a real human kid to me. I called her my sister-goat. We would bottle-feed her, put diapers on her, and keep her inside at all times. I grew up with her.

Age 5 to 10: My father's side of the family has a lot of Native American ancestors. Growing up, we were the type of white family that would call Native Americans "Indians," completely ignoring that there was a whole area of the world dedicated to actual people known as Indians. Anyway, I knew about this area because I paid attention in my classes. I grew up hearing, "We're Indian!" a lot and constantly wondering why I was not as dark as the other actual-Indian kids.

Age 6: I went to Walmart and stopped at the front of the store in order to get a sticker. This is back when Walmart had greeters and they were all old people and they always gave kids stickers and that was basically their job. Anyway, this one old man gave me a sticker and then immediately said, "I created and patented that sticky part of diapers."

Age 7: In second grade, I pooped my pants and proceeded to put the piece of poop in another kid's cubby.

Age 8: In third grade, I had a teacher named Mrs. Poddlewaddle and I would call her "Puddle of water" and one time I called her mom.

Age 9: While I was going through intermediate school, girls started growing boobs or at least hearing about them and wanting to have them. At the same time, sequin belts were very in and every girl had one. One day, a girl decided to put her sequin belt around her breasts / torso opposed to around her waist. This spread like wildfire, and soon every girl in my class was wearing their sequin belt around their boobs.

Age 11: I brought my Gwen Stefani "Love. Angel. Music. Baby." CD to school with me to show all of my fellow classmates and get called gay. However, during breakfast – before I could even show anyone – the school police officer saw me holding the CD and decided to take it from me. Later on, I was called to the principal's office and told that it was inappropriate for me to have my CD because Gwen was "half-naked" on the cover.

Age 11 to 12: In 5th and 6th grades, all of the students in my class dated each other. I'm not entirely sure what was going on, but we all knowingly dated multiple people at the same time – and we were all fine with this. Premature polyamory was running amuck in our class, but at the time we didn't have the word for it so we just laughed and said we were all dating multiple people.

Age 12: My best friend, Cassie Boyd, moved away from my hometown after 6th grade and didn't let anyone know. To this day, none of us have been able to find her online. I miss her.

Age 11-13: I slept in a La-Z Boy Recliner during these ages of my childhood. It's not that I didn't have a bed – I just preferred to sleep in a chair, apparently.

Age 13: The summer after 7th grade, I spent an exuberant amount of time staying home, playing Gaia Online, deep-frying French fries, and creating Quizzilla surveys until 6am every single night.

Age 13: My art teacher in middle school had bipolar disorder – and she was sometimes a bitch due to this. I had the opportunity to write about my school life in English class. So, of course I went in. My English teacher thought my paper was the best in the school and decided to hang it up OUTSIDE of her classroom for anyone to read. I called my art teacher a bitch with bipolar disorder in this paper.

Age 13: I tried to jailbreak my iPhone when I was 13. It broke as a result. When the Apple technicians called me, they clearly knew I had tried to jailbreak it. I replied, "Jailbreak? I'm 13."

Age 14: When I was in 8th grade, I received a t-shirt from Tennis class and a t-shirt from NJHS in the same day. Both of these instances were normal for most students who were involved in a couple different organizations at the school. However, my best friend saw that I was holding two t-shirts and decided to exclaim, "TWO T-SHIRTS IN ONE DAY?!"

Age 14: One time this weird guy wanted to have phone sex with me. So I told him to hang on, I secretly three-way called my best friend, and I made them have phone sex instead. The weird guy thought he was having phone sex with me the entire time, and my best friend just kept screaming, "TERIYAKI, YERIYAKI, TERIYAKI."

Age 14: There have been two times that I've accidentally found myself at a screamo concert. The first was when I was strolling through the park, and I found myself in the middle of a mosh pit with people pretending to bang their heads on the concrete while I wore clothes from Forever 21. The second time was at the local church, which really stirred a lot of drama in my community because everyone felt that screamo was the music of the devil.

Age 14: I have been suspended from school twice. The first time was when I said, "Fuck you!" to my tennis coach for telling me I sound like Michael Jackson. And the second time was when I was writing a poem about society for English class and I said the words, "Pricks, "Dicks," and "Boobs."

Age 15: My mom's friend thought it would be funny to give me a 365-day calendar from Sports Illustrated magazine. Each day had a female bikini model on it. I decided to rip them all out of the book, sharpie male names across their bodies, and tape them to every inch of my wall.

Age 16: I was never in band in high school, but I was pretty much the only groupie for the entire band. They invited me out to their Halloween party, which I knew was my cue to do something wild. I dressed up as an All-American bikini model, dressed in only a USA flag two-piece. However, I knew I might get in trouble for wearing just that, so I put on a Victoria Secret bathrobe and pink high heels on over my primary costume (I dubbed this the "drunk wine mom" look). At the climax of Party Rock Anthem by LMFAO, I stripped off my secondary costume and was immediately kicked out of the party.

Age 16: During Speech class Sophomore year of high school, I gave a speech on Bulimia Nervosa. I guess it really struck a cord with people because it was voted "Most Hilarious Speech" in the class.

Age 16: I attempted to go see Saw 7 in theatres. When I got to the door of the movie, they asked to see my ID. They were about to kick me out for not being 18-years-old, but suddenly two huge army men in full uniform in front of me said, "She's our daughter."

Age 17: The summer after Junior year, this girl in my school got grounded for the entire summer. She decided that the absolute best use of her time would be to go outside dressed as a clown and stand on the corner of a busy street. This immediately sent my entire town and all of its citizens into a frenzy as they tried to figure out what to do to rid the earth of this menace. She stood there for several hours each day for weeks while everyone else fought about it on Facebook.

Age 18: In the middle of Senior year, I went out to Los Angeles for Spring Break. A strange guy walked up to me on the street and asked me if I wanted to be photographed. I said, "Sure!" because I don't know anything about how to act around strangers. I found myself in his apartment while he played the SAW 1 movie score and took nude photographs of me while I wore fake rubber chains.

And since then, my life has been perfect and nothing else mattress!

DO YOU WANT TO HEAR ABOUT ALL OF THE TIMES I'VE BEEN A SHITTY PERSON?

Aside from making you read this book, there have been a whole lot of other times I've been a shitty person. Do you want to hear about all of them? They range from 6th grade to 12th grade, and I'll go in chronological order so you don't get confused and so you can see how my cruelness has maybe developed and changed. Maybe you can do a work-study on me? Would you like that? Would your university give you credit for that? Just message me. Anyway, it starts in 6th grade because I do not remember my life in detail before that year, and I was probably an even worse person. And I think I learned how to be a better person once I graduated from high school because I really don't have any stories of me being a bully after high school.

Anyway, I want to warn you that this chapter is astonishingly not funny (aside from some parts) and will definitely make you uncomfortable. You will be all, "How can a person this terrible exist and who allowed her to write a book?" Understandably. As you read this chapter, I want you to take my name out of your mind and forget entirely about how I've made you laugh at every word up to this point. I want you to view this as an opportunity to understand the perspective of the misunderstood: bullies and assholes. Or, you know, just burn this book and boycott my existence.

Okay I'm back after writing this entire chapter to engage with you in a discussion about the uncomfortable journey you are about to go on. I used several different focus groups (AKA group texts with friends) in order to gauge how well this book might be received. This chapter definitely made a lot of people uncomfortable. I thought about pushing this chapter closer to the end of the book so that I don't scare too many people off so early on, but I think I'll just explain myself instead. I want this chapter to serve as an opportunity for us to dive deep into the woes of humanity and how there's honestly a scale when it comes to being a complete dick to people. Likewise, I want us to imagine the possibility that group bullying builds some type of fucked-up morale in people. If anything, I want this chapter to serve as a think-piece and discussion on the cruelty of individuals, and even collective bullying, and how we need to have a conversation about it opposed to simply saying, "Well, that's just not right" and swearing off bullying in general. If you become uncomfortable with this chapter at any point, please move on to the next one. However, if you do so – effectively ignoring this chapter, – I want you to also ask yourself whether or not your uncomfortability and, thus, silence is allowing this phenomenon of group cruelty and layered bullying to continue. But lol, no pressure or anything.

6th Grade: There was this girl named Eomely in sixth grade, but she went by "Emily" – it confused the hell out of everyone because Eemely clearly doesn't look like Emily, but she insisted that this was correct. Anyway, we would later find out that she was from a broken family that was constantly moving from town-to-town. So, yeah, her life wasn't ideal or anything. She was hella awkward and heavy-set and no one liked her – not even the teachers. The students would constantly team up in order to pull pranks on her or call her ugly. The fucked-up part? It was, like, great for classroom morale and it sparked teamwork. We were all happy and having a great time and looked like we could be on the cover of a magazine about the best classroom in the world. Of course, all at the expense of Eemely.

Well, my best friend and I decided that we would be the ringleaders in these covert operations to make Eemely's life a living hell. I remember this one time: she went to the bathroom and we decided that the absolute funniest thing to do at the time would be to steal all of her writing utensils and then pretend like she must have taken them to the bathroom with her when she got back. She walked back and forth between the bathroom and the classroom sooooo many times that day. At the time, we felt like we were doing her a favor – she got some exercise. If Fitbit gadgets would have been around back then, we would have claimed to be doing her the service of helping her get her steps in. So, you know, perspective. I would give you more examples, but honestly I probably blocked out that part of my life after I decided to never treat someone like that ever again.

Well, after being at our school for about half a year, the counselor came into our homeroom and decided to tell all of us that it was time for Eemely to move… yet again. I'm pretty sure the teacher continued to teach as the counselor said this because we really did not fucking care about this girl – it was so sad. The next day, the teachers literally DANCED IN THE HALLWAY BECAUSE EEMELY WAS GONE. I don't even remember her being the kind of student that teachers hate; she literally wasn't a bad person or mean or anything that made a student stick out. She was a goddamn normal student with a wildly depressing home-life. But I guess the lesson here is: teachers are also bullies and assholes, and we will never be able to escape people like that, and I hope Eemely isn't, like, fucked up now or something.

8th Grade: Okay, so I take back everything I said about this chapter not being funny because this story is actually kind of funny, if you ignore everything bad about it and turn your head and squint your eyes. Anyway, I was walking with my best friend (different asshole best friend, equally as terrible and amazing) into the middle school one morning. I was scanning my eyes around the perimeters to see whom I could make fun of, intimidate, and bully into submission. Suddenly, I see a 7th grade student wheeling around airport luggage AS HIS BACKPACK. Score! (To be fair, I had also never seen anyone carry a bag in any other way than on their back / on their shoulder. So this kid was weird as fuck. Also don't scream, "He was probably poor and couldn't afford any other type of bag!" because duh! That was obviously the case. I didn't give a shit.)

Now, I didn't go up to him and directly bully him or anything. In fact, it's likely that he never even experienced my bullying whatsoever. I decided to simply laugh and say, "He's thinks this is an airport! What if this was an airport?" To which my best friend said, "Do it." I proceeded to tell everyone in the school that we were now in an airport and that the class time would be vacation locations and the passing periods would be plane rides. Every single day, I would go home and write down eight different countries (one for each class period at school) on at least fifty different pieces of paper for the next day. That was the vacation schedule for the day. I would give them out to people during breakfast, and everyone would talk about it all day. Luckily no one figured out that I clearly didn't know how to use a copier.

    Anyway, we did this for about five months and then I got bored with this indirect secret bullying performance that had way too many layers to it that I just decided to, I don't know, read a book or something like a normal student. Or I could…

    8th Grade: … make my best friend believe her boyfriend was cheating on her with a Katy Perry knock-off. Yeah, I didn't let much time pass between these stunts because, guess what? MySpace. A separate best friend (the one from the Eemely story) and I discovered that we could be completely different people on MySpace because there are no rules and no one cares about the online world! Our creative minds were able to run free on this website because there were absolutely no consequences back then.

    We both created fake profiles depicting 16-year-old girls who were best friends and worked at McDonald's together. I unknowingly chose Katy Perry (before she was famous) as my profile picture because she looked like a real punk bitch in it – here, I'll show you:

This was, like, right before her "One Of The Boys" album. Anyway, that's not the point. The point is that it was sort of believable given the amount of time me and my best friend put into developing these characters, that no one knew Katy Perry, and that we were all dumbasses in middle school. So, we played around with the profiles for a couple of months and made them interact with our real MySpace accounts and yadda yadda so that everyone at our school would eventually believe that these girls were real and totally worked at our local McDonald's. Plus, they were cooler because they were 16!

      At around the same time, my other best friend was pretty much ignoring me and all of her friends because she had a new boyfriend who she was totally in love with or something dumb. It was the grossest thing I had ever encountered. I decided: why not utilize my new fake MySpace account in order to bring the most good to the greatest amount of people. If I were to break them up in a way that wouldn't come back on me and, thus, release her back to all of her loved ones… then maybe I could feel like I'm doing SOMETHING nice and ethical with my life. That's what utilitarianism is all about, right? So I decided to message her from my fake Katy-Perry-at-McDonald's account and tell her, "hey gurl!! not to upset u or any thing but ur boyfrend came into mickky deeees yesturday && he gave me his #. i found out hes datin u so i just wanted u 2 kno that we made out!!!!" It took this girl a quick second to break up with her boyfriend. I'm talking MILLISECONDS. Anyway, I guess everyone else was happy in the end.

10th Grade: When I was transitioning from 9th to 10th grade, I started a relationship with this guy who I bagged while he was bagging my groceries at the local grocery store. I bought a potato because I thought he was cute and wanted him to bag it. One day while I was in Chemistry class, one of my best friends (who sat behind me) poked me on the back and handed me a note that said, "Hey, I know we're not supposed to be writing notes during class, but your boyfriend sent me nudes last night." Of course, I was simultaneously horrified and ecstatic at the same time. Horrified because I was being cheated on, and ecstatic because I knew this was my cue to execute yet another dramatically long prank at the expense of someone else.

Immediately after class let out, I told my best friend that we had to devise a plan that would humiliate my now-ex-boyfriend, but ONLY with us being in on the joke. Therefore, no humans were actually emotionally harmed in the making. The ex-boyfriend lived in the town next door and no one in my school actually knew who he was – so we had free reign to say whatever the fuck we wanted, with the understanding that literally no one else would know what we were talking about. We decided to make up a rumor about him having a gastrointestinal disease that made him leak poop. We started telling everyone we knew that I was no longer in a relationship anymore because "Evan leaks poop" and it just strained (and stained) our relationship too much. I gave sob stories about how I would have to go into Walmart and buy multiple boxes of adult diapers just so my boyfriend wouldn't be embarrassed. I told everyone who would listen about how hard I had it when my boyfriend would accidentally shit on me while we were holding hands at the movies. I even had discussions with my teachers about my enhanced knowledge of the gastrointestinal tract and how I only knew so much about the diseases found in the stomach and colon because I cared so deeply about this poor guy who ultimately ended up cheating on me (when in reality I only knew so much because of Wikipedia). It was great! I was the martyr in the story I created, and Evan leaked poop.

Please continue reading this book even though you should be pissed off at me.

I promise everything else is funny and not gross.

MEN IN UNIFORM, THE MUSICAL

Speaking of nude modeling (yeah, that's a segue from two chapters ago!), I want to discuss the amount of men in my life whom I've had wildly inappropriate and uncomfortable relationships with. Most of these men were in positions of privilege and authority, which is great for me, but not so much for anyone else whatsoever. I love a man in uniform, and I will always gladly be taken advantage of because I understand that I have no advantages and, really, it's all disadvantages. Anyway, that Los Angeles photographer who took pictures of my genitals was only one man in a long list of men who were exceptionally older, yet not wiser than me.

The first time I encountered a man of significant age disparity and authority looking to take my tiny body for a ride I wasn't yet tall enough for was when I sucked off a Peace Officer during the school hours – but that's just a fun preamble. The first time it really mattered to my wellbeing was when I was exposed to a naked Police Officer masturbating in his own house. I didn't want to be. He didn't want me to be. But it happened. And now it's going in this book. I was 16-years-old at the time and, instead of doing what happened, I was supposed to be picking up my friend's friend, Carly. Carly was this punk girl who didn't have calling on her cell phone, so I had to rely on her pretty poor texting skills. I drove all the way out into the country, where houses are scarce and the addresses are pretty weird, apparently. I arrived at the exact address Carly had texted me. Now, at the time, I was an extremely nervous person, so of course I texted her back telling her I was there – I didn't even knock. "Come on in," said Carly. I wasn't about to just walk into a stranger's house, so I waited five minutes. I walked in anyway. I was immediately in a living room with a dog and all of the lights on. I waited for five minutes. I went back outside. "No one was inside," I replied. "Just come to the back." Surely Carly had arms and legs – I have no clue why she couldn't' go to the door herself. Whatever. So, I went back in. I walked past the dog, out of the living room, and into the kitchen. There was still no one there. I saw a room just past the kitchen with a light on. I walked up to the room only to experience the climax of this story. Are you ready? This dude was just lying in his bed fully naked with one of those weird laptop stands over him and his laptop on top of that. His right hand was on his dick and I can only assume porn images were emitting from the screen in front of him. I immediately hushed, "I'm sorry" and started to walk fast towards the door. "YOU'RE LUCKY MY DOG DIDN'T ATTACK YOU," he screamed as his dog literally just sat in the same exact spot it had been since I walked in the first time. "What are you doing here?" "I'm looking for Carly." "Carly is in the BACK house!"

   Anyway, suffice to say, Carly lived in the house two houses behind the house I was in, and apparently they all had the same address? Yeah, that isn't exactly something everyone assumes, Carly. Anyway, I found out he was a cop because when I finally got to Carly's real house, the cop had already phoned her dad and he was all, "That guy's a cop! He could have you arrested!" As if I wasn't already mentally arrested enough by having to be exposed to him masturbating. Weirdly enough, I was still able to take Carly – someone I didn't even know personally at all – with me to my friend's house.

In the case that Carly is reading this book and has not learned her lesson, I would just like to teach her that "Come on in!" is not a good substitute for actually being a good person and opening the door for your guests. Likewise, "Just come to the back" should not be said when three houses have the exact same address. I'm sure we can all agree with this, so Carly: please get your shit together.

A couple of years after that, I was at a volunteer convention where several thousand students gathered to talk about being gay or something – I don't know. Anyway, I was entirely interested in one thing and one thing only: old dick. My eye candy: the 60-year-old International Director of the entire organization (one of the biggest in the world)

I was at the convention for. Lucky for me, rumor had it that he had a hankering for young pussy and clearly wasn't afraid to be fired for the near-despicable (yet godly to me) acts he was supposedly committing. I found out where he was staying at the convention hotel and headed down to his room around 1am one night. He answered the door, and I immediately just walked in and told him that he was the hottest fox I had ever seen. Long story short: we had sex that night. Yay!

Then I moved to a new city for university and decided that I would like to engage in nude modeling again. I posted a couple of Craigslist ads and eventually got a bite from a professional nude photographer. I met with him at a local coffee shop, as two artists do, and we discussed what I would need to do in order to be the best damn nude model he had ever seen. Here's a list of just a couple of things I guess you're supposed to do if you want your pussy to pop and your skin to be flawless:

- Take multivitamins,

- Exercise,

- Drink only water,

- Don't masturbate or have sex for at least six weeks before the shoot,

- Get your hair cut how you'd like it about a week before the shoot,

- Etc.

    And it was all set! I was gonna shove multivitamins and water down my throat while exercising and not masturbating until it was time to get my hair cut like a sexy porn star for the camera again. I had kept in constant contact with him – normal things like how his wife was doing, what kind of shoots he'd been accomplishing, etc. – and was determined to continue my secret modeling career with sketchy men for as long as I could. Then he lost his leg. I don't know how, why, when, where, or what, but my nude photographer lost his leg, thus preventing us from doing a shoot. It happened a couple of weeks before we were supposed to work together (I didn't even get my hair cut!): I was on Facebook and I saw a post that had a picture of him in a hospital bed attached. He was surrounded by family and one less leg. Of course he never contacted me about canceling the shoot or making it up, and I wasn't expecting him to. I, although an amateur in nude modeling, understood clearly that if a photographer loses one of his legs, your shoot might never happen. It took me three years to do another nude shoot, and I'm still triggered by nudity to this day – and by triggered, I mean I laugh (not at him) and remember this story.

While in university, I learned about those huge clock towers that almost every university has that play the time and ding and dong and whatever. I guess they're called Carillons? And there's a professional at the top of every major university clock tower that helps ding the dong. And I wanted to ding the dong of whoever was responsible for it. One day, I found out about the man who stood atop the clock tower and forced us to know what time it was. And he was just my type: old. I made sure he knew who I was and one day, he invited me into the office that controlled the clock and the carillon. We had sex in the office that day.

Also in university, I matched with one of my county's judges on a dating app. I didn't hook up with him, but one time he did pretend to be his "wife" and text me from his phone. "She" said, "This is his wife – don't text him again." And that was a really great prank by an elected official.

    The scene for this next story is in a club. I was at a not-so-popular club at 6pm because my friend was bartending and it was Taco Tuesday. This meant free tacos, which meant I suddenly had the ability to teleport to them. When I arrived, this older guy in medical scrubs wouldn't stop hitting on me. I told him I didn't drink alcohol (true at the time), but that he could keep telling the bartender to give me water if he really wanted to be my servant. I also told him that I happened to be abstinent at the time (also true), so there was really no reason for him to continue talking to me. I'm not sure what else he wanted, so – not knowing anything about 6pm club culture, apparently – I asked him the ~weirdest~ question I could come up with: "Do you have any cocaine?" He didn't even have to think about it. He said, "Yes" as fast as he could, as if he was carrying cocaine at all times and just waiting for someone to ask him about it. I – again, knowing nothing about the community I was imposing myself in – stupidly tried to call his bluff and proceeded with, "Well, if you do, you can snort it off of my body." Never before have I seen a nurse pull little baggies of white powder out of their scrub pockets. It was like I was *in* Nurse Jackie. Now, when I promise something to somebody, I will ensure it happens, if only to prove to myself that I can keep my promises. He led me to the handicap stall in the women's restroom (I guess it didn't matter that he was in there), as if he had done it dozens of times before, and poured the bags over my stomach. Blah, blah, blah, there were two people having sex in the stall next to us while it was happening, blah, blah. And that was it! Sometimes you never know what situation God is going to get you into each day!

I did study abroad in Italy. There were several prominent universities participating in programs while I was there, which meant that there were a lot of old male professors looking to have sex with students in a foreign county. (This is always the case. It's almost cultural.) Anyway, a 70-year-old Law professor from a university not far away from mine decided to find me on Facebook and message the hell out of me.

Unfortunately, he wasn't that sexual. I guess he just wanted to have a bona fide relationship with someone fifty years younger than him. He took me on the fanciest date in Italy and I basked in the glory of knowing that I was about to snag the sweetest of sugar daddies. I think he's dead now.

    Does anybody want to adapt what you just read into a musical?

SEX!!!!!

Now that I've told you about my sex life with older men, I might as well just discuss my sex life in general – and also the mishaps along the way. Put on a condom! Because you're about to get FUCKED.

There are two separate times that I've contracted Sexually Transmitted Infections (STIs) – but I'm only going to talk about one of those times. Can you guess which STI I contracted? Am I able to make a poll on here? Here's what I'm going to do: I'm going to include a poll after this sentence, and you circle which STI you think I contracted in the summer of 2015 before I give you the answer:

- Gonorrhea
- Syphilis
- Crabs
- Chlamydia

The answer is CRABS! Did you get it right? Do you want a prize? Get ahold of me and let me know how you did on this quiz.

In case you were wondering, I did not contract this STI from any of the old men I described in the previous chapter. In fact, I didn't contract it from anyone whatsoever. Crabs is the only STI that you can contract without being sexual or intimate or getting anywhere near another human being. In the summer of 2015, I was traveling the United States probably being a hoe or volunteering – it's a toss up, – so I was staying in a lot of different hotels and dorm rooms. The next thing I knew, I had crabs. I went to see a doctor about it, and they informed me that I most likely contracted this STI from sleeping in a bed in which someone else who had crabs slept in up to three weeks prior to me. That's how wild this STI is. Anyone could contract it at ANY GIVEN TIME, and then for the rest of their life they have to tick the YES box for "Have you ever contracted an STI?" at the doctor's office.

      Now I want to shift gears a little bit to discuss how prostitution is totally legal in Amsterdam and how I can look at women's titties in front of a crowd of people for just a couple bucks. Sounds great, right? Unless the peep show you attend reminds you of philosophers and horror films. I recently ran away to Amsterdam without telling anyone and purchased a ticket to a peep show for a measly two euros (much cheaper than when I pay women in the United States to flash me). I walked into the small room that they led me to and the screen in front of me immediately went from black to transparent, like a window. I saw a woman situated in the center of the room in front of me, on a bed that was spinning in a circular motion. I noticed there were eleven other small rooms like the one I was in all linked together making a circle around this woman and her bed. I could see the faces of exclusively-men at each of their respective windows. I realized that the woman performing the peep show on the bed in the center of the room could see us just as we could see her – and we could all see each other. This already sounds like some weird fucked-up horror movie, right? Maybe Hostel 3 mixed with Saw 6 and also the feeling you get before someone Human Centipedes you?

    Anyway, this situation sort of reminded me of panopticons. Basically, this French philosopher by the name of Paul-Michel Foucault heavily invoked this theory and educational movement centered around people gathering in the shape of a literal circle, or buildings known as panopticons. He pushed this interesting commentary about circular institutions being superior to any other type of institution, with the vision of everyone being easily observed and understood. However, this idea only gets creepy when you realize that the original creation of a panopticon – by English philosopher and social theorist Jeremy Bentham – was thought-up in order to lessen the workload of the prison system, putting a single prison guard in the center of a circular prison and having this guard be able to monitor every single prisoner at once. Although, yes, it is impossible for the guard to be able to monitor all locations at once, it still leaves the prisoners understanding that at any given time he can swivel in his chair and view them in an instant; thus enforcing a self-sustaining prison system where prisoners control their own behavior. It's the ultimate watchman's dream. Although Foucault utilized this theory in an educational sense – stating that we should create circular classroom structures where students make up the circle and the professor is in the middle, – it still stands that the use of panopticons was created purely for monitoring behaviors and improving self-governing systems.

    That's why when I saw that peep show performer in the center of the room and all of those gross male faces in a circle, I immediately started laughing. To the point, where I could not possibly stop. The performer saw me laughing and decided to focus her attention on me. Then I attempted to be super serious, so I crossed my arms and made a face that meant business. She decided to mimic me, so she crossed her arms, as well. She was this beautiful naked woman sitting on a spinning bed looking at me and mimicking my moves. And all I could think about was a social theory and horror movies. Anyway, this is definitely what Bentham and

Foucault envisioned.

    I have no segue for this next story, but I have a guy out in New Orleans that I regularly fist every time I find myself out there. And by fist, I mean I stick half of my entire arm up his asshole / body, at that point. I met him on a dating app several years back, and he is in the scene of people who love to be fisted sexually. However, for me, this act is never sexual; I platonically do this for him because he is my friend and I like creating stories that I can someday write into a book. One time before our usual fisting session, we went out to a voyeuristic, kink-infested nightclub in order to get in the mood, as he would put it. Here: I'll just put you in the mindset.
    Imagine you arrive at a nightclub. The rule about this nightclub is that there are no phones allowed because the entire club has to be dark in order for people to feel more comfortable engaging in their kinks. The only light allowed emits from the television behind the bartenders, and it exclusively plays porn of guys butt-chugging. The bathrooms are off-limits for anything bathrooms are inherently used for, and age

does not seem to matter to anyone. As you walk around the club, you find cool gadgets that you've never seen before, and swings that are meant for anything but that action. The mid-2000s pop music overhead is muffled by the multitude of moaning heard from the mouths of at least a dozen people getting it on right in front of you. Immediately, you wonder how legal this place truly could be, but you don't care because it transcends you to a realm not policed by laws against the sexually oppressed. Initially, it takes you a good hour to fully comprehend what exactly you're doing there, and once you leave it takes another hour to figure out how to live in the outside world again.

      Does this place appeal to you? Could you see yourself going here before a fisting session? Do you want to talk about it at a later time?

      If you would prefer an experience a little more intimate / not as hardcore, I would suggest engaging in orgasmic meditation. Essentially, this form of meditation ensures you become in-tune with your body and the sexuality of all individuals involved in the session. These sessions usually consist of at least two-dozen people and range from being solely verbally sexual (telling people what you would do to them sexually) to tease games to full on hand job orgies. The intensity of the session depends on how much money you pay the orgasmic meditation service. For a couple of hundred dollars, you will find yourself slipping your fingers into the vagina of another woman, focusing primarily on the upper right quadrant of her clitoris. Meanwhile, soothing music plays and all eyes are shut in order to enhance the sexual senses. However, if you choose to simply "check out" a session, they will have you arrive in a room filled with several other people that you are supposed to get to know and discuss your sexuality with. As you can probably guess by now, this service almost exclusively appeals to old men and people who never have sex. Therefore, you really just find yourself trapped inside a room with a bunch of people who are yelling their sexual desires at you and trying to find you after the session to hook up without having to pay. Oh well!

Or you could go the Air Sex route. Air Sex is exactly how it sounds – like playing the Air Guitar but with sex. This new form of entertainment was invented back in 2006 when a group of bored Japanese men in Tokyo discovered that they don't need girlfriends to have exciting (air) sex lives. It was quickly appropriated by the United States, and now there's a traveling Air Sex group that goes all over the country. When you arrive at a showing, you are asked if you would like to participate during the show. This results in a bunch of strangers humping the air (talk about dry) on a bona fide theatre stage in front of hundreds of spectators. No one touches and consent is not needed. The show lasts for a couple of hours, and afterwards you wonder how that was particularly different from the 2008 film Australia.

    All right! That's my chapter about sex! You can take your condom off now!

DATING IS SIMULTANEOUSLY BOTH AN ART FORM AND NOT REAL

Here's the thing: dating is weird and everyone seems to be doing it. But why? Literally why? Our crippling loneliness? Social grooming? Just for fun? I truly don't understand it, so I see it as an art form that everyone has decided to engage in. It is the single biggest and longest art movement that this world has ever seen, so of course I want to discuss it from a philosophical standpoint – possibly how it's completely imaginary. And I would also like to give you some tips on how to go about performing this fake art piece with another human being.

First, you need to download a dating app – any will do. Next you need to think of a bio (short for "biography") for your dating profile. A bio is something everyone will see, so it needs to represent you – or, you know, not at all. Here are a couple of bios that I have used for myself in the past:

- In prison. If you want to meet me, you have to give them my ID number. It's #002481. Don't tell them that I have a phone in here – just say you're my brother or something.

- Looking for a drinking partner! And my parents! Where are my parents ☹

- Check out my website! www.pornhub.com

- In a committed relationship with GOD. We decided we're gonna try an open relationship.

- I'm not bi so why would I have a bio…………

- Thank you for visiting my dating profile! How was your trip? Can I get you anything – maybe a cup of tea or a snack? I got some whales in t- Oh, Whales – they're sort of like Goldfish but a different bran- Oh, okay. Yeah, just the tea? Perfect. Well, make yourself at home!

- Hi! Name is Ashley. I love hiking, dogs, and traveling. Let's grab a beer or two! Let's get several beers. Let's get drunk on beer. Let's buy a brewing machine together. Let's rob a beer distillery. Let's get so drunk on beer that we burn down a liquor store. Let's die in that fire while covered in beer. Cheers! Message me and get to know me!

Once you've filled out your bio and profile, you can now start chatting with other individuals. People on dating apps typically have the brainpower of a 5-year-old, so don't expect too many conversations that last beyond "Hi!" and "Nothing much." But for those times that the stars align and you do chat with someone who knows what a book is, you will want to plan the perfect first date. And that's where I come in. I'll be your personal dating concierge / first date curator. Here are some first date examples:

- Have him take you to the collective funeral for twelve different first responders who died fighting an explosion. Make sure every United Stated President except for Bill Clinton is in attendance. This will make him fall in love with you and then abuse you two years later, guaranteed!

- Go to Chili's and order the 2 for $20 together to save money. Make this a tradition so that when y'all eventually break up, you continue to order the 2 for $20 to-go for yourself and spread it over the next four meals.

- Agree to meet in a coffee shop and write-up exactly how the relationship is going to happen. Ensure that it ends with him angrily creating a series of eight poems about you for his poetry course, and that his professor likes the poems so much that she suggests he apply for the best MFA grad programs in the country.

- Go to IKEA to rip-off the movie "500 Days of Summer" by pretending to be a married couple shopping for furniture. Only, instead of falling in love eventually, make sure he absolutely hates you within a six-month timeframe. Then watch Finding Dory together afterwards.

- Take him to the house you grew up in and introduce him to every single one of your family members. That way, when he ghosts you in the middle of your relationship, it's really awkward for your entire family.

Now after y'all have had your first date, you need to make sure that he doesn't ghost you, like that last guy on the first date list. If he truly likes you, he probably won't ghost you – but this could also not be the case. Sometimes guys ghost you because they like you TOO much. Anyway, in order to avoid being ghosted, you need to understand what ghosting looks like, and how to spot a ghoster. I'll tell you about some of my experiences with ghosting to help you in your journey. Ghosting can take many different forms:

- The Sophomore in university whom I was dating as a Sophomore in high school.

- The guy who took me on a 16-hour date.

- My boyfriend, who I had been in a relationship with for two months.

- My dating concierge.

- A prisoner I attempted to become friends with in high school.

- The Orange Is The New Black actor who had me purchase a plane ticket to Amsterdam so we could see the premiere of his new film together, but never showed up.

If you do find that various men you meet on dating apps are continually ghosting you, then a good rule of thumb is to just date as many of them as possible, as fast as possible. This is known as The Ancient Middle-School Courtship System of Hyperspeed Serial Dating. I'll explain.

Every time I blink an eye, it seems my friends are dating completely different people than they were just a second ago! Who can keep up! Hyperspeed Serial Dating, often defined as that time in middle school when you would date a new person every couple of class periods, is the act of being able to date someone else the second your previous relationship ends. It is a cycle and doesn't have a clear end goal or an emotional appeal whatsoever. The people who often engage in Hyperspeed Serial Dating are required to have a VERY LOW to nonexistent level of empathy and no romantic vision for the future. Thus, they are often expressed as the 4% of sociopaths in our society – but this is not proven and just rude to state! On the contrary, I think these people are not only preserving a rare phenomenon that we all thought stopped after middle school because of the assumed increase in emotional maturity that comes with age (guess not!), but also being modern-day heroes by showcasing to other people that having no empathy can get you laid quick and easy! Quick and easy sex wrapped up in the pretty bow that is a *relationship* is the sneakiest way to cover up the fact that you're really just sleeping with a bunch of people! Why not just say that you're sleeping with a bunch of people? Literally no one cares! Hyperspeed Serial Daters have mastered the art of tricking society into reframing what indiscriminate promiscuous sex with tons of people really is: romantic!

So forget that emotional turn-around! If he ghosts you, get right back on the wagon within seconds and date someone new for a minute or two! You may be saying, "But Ashley, I have the correct amount of emotional maturity, and I don't have the luxury of being a borderline sociopath!" Well, all that changes now! I suggest you create a public DoodlePoll indicating the times in which you plan to be single. You can have the guys on your dating apps sign up for a time slot (no more than 2 hours; as little as

15 minutes!) in order to date you. Tell them they're allowed to spread the news of your new relationship to their friends and family – that way, when you break up with them and have a new guy within seconds, their friends and family will give them the empathy you never did.

However, don't forget why we're here: because dating is fake and makes no sense whatsoever. That's why I'm ultimately proposing that none of us date each other anymore. It's over, y'all! It's canceled! Get your divorce papers in line and ghost your significant other! It's 2017 – why are we still engaged in this faux art movement? It's 2017 – stop dating each other. It's 2017 – relationships aren't a thing anymore.

I went to the club the other day and a guy came up to me and the stranger standing to my left. This guy asked, "How long have y'all been together?" to which I replied, "Two years." Then me and my new boyfriend of two-years, apparently, proceeded to pretend that we were in a bona fide two-year long-term relationship, and none of it mattered. Now, THAT'S a metaphor. That's the crutch of a philosophy about how dating is not real. You can look at any single human being and decide right then and there exactly how long you have been dating and whether or not you *are* dating. And guess what: none of it matters at all! So why don't we cut the bullshit and move on to more important things, like technological singularity or planting trees? Surely we could be using our energy a lot more wisely than this.

    Oh my god, did this chapter even make any sense at all?

WILD COLLEGE STORIES!

The first thing they gave me when I arrived on my university for my first year as a college student was an invitation to be put on suicide watch. *Whoa, what a strong way to start a chapter, Ashley.* Calm down – I wasn't actually suicidal. I guess some dickweed turned me in to the university police because my twitter sounded a little depressing. In reality, I just used to love to joke about suicide. That's what was funny back then. Anyway, if that doesn't serve as a proper preamble to how my university career / life was going to play out, I don't know what else will suffice. For the next four years after that moment, it seemed to just be one wild college story after the next until I found myself stumbling across the commencement stage wondering how I had truly done it.

But before I get into some of the stories that I am personally responsible for, I want to discuss one that keeps me wondering and on my toes to this day: the dreaded roommate situation.

For my first two months in college, I had this diagnosed-psychotic roommate who was the absolute worst person I have ever met to this day. Let me just portray her by writing a résumé for her. Maybe you can relate to these situations! (Warning: this is initially going to sound like I'm just complaining about normal college stuff, but I promise it gets more wild.)

ASHLEY'S ROOMMATE

[ADDRESS] [TELEPHONE] [EMAIL]

OBJECTIVE:
- To destroy Ashley's life.

SKILLS:
- *Leaving Unwanted Items In Inappropriate Places*

I'm an expert at not noticing where I'm putting things, and I think any place in the apartment is good enough to be a sink or a trashcan. Before Ashley moved in, I made sure to decorate the place a little bit. The two plastic cups, a glass bowl, and a metal spoon that I left laying around the toilet surprised her. I also decided to leave my high heels on the sink permanently, never unpack anything (but ensure it's left in the way of others), and prematurely decorate the living room with peace signs and pink zebra print even though the other roommates believe it's inconsiderate and tacky.

- Consuming As Much Space As Possible

Being a bitch, I know a lot about taking everything for myself and ensuring no one else is comfortable. I have personally placed my various amounts of beauty products all over both sink counters, filled up both the cabinet and the prescription compartment, along with the entire shower caddie and the four corners of the tub. Thus leaving no room for Ashley's stuff at all.

- Using Items That Are Obviously Not Mine

Even though I have an abundance of my own bathroom supplies that take up every inch of the bathroom, I still like to use Ashley's. I once used her mouthwash and misplaced it outside of the bathroom. Unfortunately, she found it and retrieved it. I have also used her electric shaver. Again, she found it inside of the bathtub with my shaving cream and took it back.

- Being Unbelievably Disruptive Even When I'm Not Home

I'm a pro at keeping people awake 24/7. In fact, I never turn my music off and I keep it on loud even when I'm away from the apartment. Because my computer and television are right up against Ashley's wall, I keep my xBox Live on constantly in tune with my music. I also make sure to turn every light on, especially after Ashley turns them off because even though I pretend to pay the bills, I still want to run up the electricity. Since I don't go to school or do anything, I can do this ALL night long.

- Demanding Conditions That Apply To Everyone Except Me

When I'm comfortable with being inconsiderate, but not when other people are, I have to convey it in inappropriate ways. I did exactly this by writing "flush toilet" with a sharpie on mine and Ashley's toilet. Even though Ashley always flushes and I have never seen any of her remains in the water, I still think this needs to be said. However, I will definitely be leaving unflushed maxi pads, feces, urine, and hair in the toilet because the rules do not apply to me.

- Forcing Others To Do My Chores

Upon the other roommates moving in, I filled the sink up with dirty dishes, left two empty pizza boxes on the apartment floor, filled up all of the trashcan, and littered personal belongings all over my roommates' areas. Even after my roommates' first month of living there, these obscenities were still not taken care of, forcing my roommates to do my dirty work in order to even wash their own dishes or throw away their own trash.

- Making People Believe My Family Is dead

I can easily and unregretfully make people believe my father, mother, and siblings are all dead. This is not true, for I post about all of them on my Facebook and have even tagged two of my real, alive sisters that look the same as me and are from the same city in a post I made. However, when it comes to Ashley, I just have to make her, her mother, and her aunt believe my whole family is dead and that I am all alone in the world, which I have explicitly verbally stated to them.

- *Committing Crimes*

Although my complex doesn't allow pets, that doesn't stop me from owning a giant dog and two hamsters. However, I can't keep ALL of these animals in my room. And even though Ashley wanted to put a television on the TV stand in the living room, I think my hamsters are more deserving, even though I'll eventually cannibalize, kill, and throw them off of a balcony. Oh, I almost forgot: I told the roommates that I was going to kill my hamsters. Even though they thought it was a joke, I successfully did it the next day. Ashley discovered this when I allowed the surviving hamster to become a cannibal and eat its partner, because I never fed them. Upon this discovery, I had to get rid of the evidence, so I threw both hamsters off of our third story balcony. Ashley later found their bodies.

- *Committing Crimes, Continued*

Keeping animals illegally hostage and killing them aren't my only strong suits – I also don't legally live in my apartment! Because I don't go to school, I cannot legally live in my student-housing complex, but they don't know that I don't go to school! Within a week of Ashley moving in, they've convicted me because I owe them $1,200! They took the key to the apartment, the key to my room, and the key to the mailbox, but that doesn't mean they have to know I still stay there. So my roommates don't find out, I lie to each of them about each other. And if I need in the apartment? I literally just break the front door down even though Ashley stated she would be home in 15 minutes. I take pride in my impatience and ability to break things that only temporarily and partially belong to me.

- *Neglecting To Pay The Bills*

Because I put the bills in my name against the wishes of anyone else, I receive them in the mailbox that I don't have access to. Therefore, our utilities sometimes threaten to get shut off. Oops. I usually give them about a 1-2 day notice, if they're lucky, about the bills, and even though they pay them on time, I still like to hoard their money and not pay the bills. I don't tell them this because, I mean, they'll eventually find out when electricity and gas get shut off. I needed to pay my phone bill with their money first, though!

EDUCATION:
- *None*

My ability to attend a community college for more than the maximum amount of time is something I am extremely proud of. So much that I actually decided I wasn't going to go to school at all anymore, but still make my apartment believe I'm a student. My illegal stay shows my ability to deceive.

EXPERIENCE:

Ashley is not the first roommate I have done this to. If you look through my Facebook history, you will see that I stole money and a can of Febreze from an old roommate. When confronted with the theft, I simply changed my number and moved.

My Facebook posts include the following:
- *It feels good not to love anybody.*
- *Part of being a bitch is that I don't give a shit what you have to say.*
- *Nothing like old-fashion penis in your face.*

Anyway, that was the time of my life and I loved every second of it. I am eternally grateful for her. However, she really fucked me up and I spent the rest of my university life trying to emulate her sporadic behaviors. Here are a bunch of stories about the things I did while in university:

- I hung out with a bunch of punk individuals who were throwing an "art party." I didn't know any of them, and I still can't remember how I ended up there, but before I knew it I wanted to desperately impress them. Given their background, the things they were saying, and how hardcore they seemed to want to be, I decided that I, too, would become a punk. While they were creating art out of random items, I went to the bathroom and used a razor blade to cut part of upper arm and collect some blood. I came back and started panting a children's coloring book I had found with my blood. They all freaked out and kicked me out of their party.

- One summer, I went to this historic site in another state. I'm not going to get into the specifics because they are not important. What's important is that I was almost kidnapped by Australians. Me and these Australian people had the same end-goal while at the site, and they asked me if I wanted to get in their car so we could go accomplish our goal together. The entire time, they joked about me being their hostage and kidnapping me. Luckily I was video recording the entire situation, and so they let me go.

- I was in business school for the summer back in 2015, but dropped out and then lived in Los Angeles for a month. While there, an old guy tried to hit me up on a dating app. I was particularly sad on this day and so I was walking from West Hollywood to Hollywood and did not feel like chatting to anyone. He told me that he would like to drive by me and just wave. I thought that was hilarious, so I agreed. However, he ended up pulling his car to the side of the road and expecting me to chat with him. Dick! That wasn't part of our agreement! Anyway, I got in his car and we drove away because I was too sad to care. I found out that he was the former most successful chiropractor in LA, and that he left that business to do spiritual healing for pets.

- I sort of got married to this stranger at my university the same day that we met. I say sort of because we were not legally married or anything, but we did go down to the County Clerk's office and pay a good amount of money in order to get the marriage certificate and all of the required items. We were then put in a governmental database. However, we didn't want to ruin our lives just yet, so of course we didn't finalize the marriage. I still have the certificate though.

- While in university, I constantly got told I must have been on a lot of drugs, but I never even drank alcohol. So anyway, I guess I'm just generally destructive and stupid without the aid of any type of substance.

Anyway, I guess this chapter wasn't truly about my wild college stories and was more about how I just really needed to vent about my old roommate. Who knew this is what I needed? Thank y'all for being there for me. You can go now.

A CHAPTER IN WHICH I LIVE-REVIEW MANY MIXTAPES

A Letter Addressed To The Individuals Who Created These Mixtapes:

Hi mister rappers,

I promise that I am not making fun of your careers or livelihoods, and only wish the best for you and your rhymes. Everything mentioned in this chapter is strictly for comedic purposes, and even if I do truly think what I say, well maybe you can take it as a good music critique. Like Pitchfork, maybe? Likewise, this could be taken as me promoting you, so I want to give you the opportunity to maybe think about it like that. Please don't be angry with me.

Ashley Jane Richardson

If you're not one of the three rappers I discuss and dissect in this chapter, then you really didn't have to read that little intro on the previous page. But you probably did because I gave no warning. Sorry!

So, I LOVE mixtapes. To the point of having a custom shirt made that states, "I WILL BUY YOUR MIXTAPE" in the case that I go to a big city and nobody thinks I want their mixtape. While visiting any city, I will quite literally attach myself to any moving vehicle and cruise through downtown while I create loud harpy-like sirens with my mouth indicating to rappers that I am in their nearby vicinity and would love one mixtape, please! I have drawn up the business plans for a physical store that acts in between a record store and a fast food chain in which you order / purchase a mixtape, with the connection being that you can either purchase an Already-Been-Made Mixtape or order one to be made right then and there. Point is: Mixtapes are cool and underrated.

Therefore, it's no surprise that I have at least a dozen plastic CD cases from Walmart with blank CDs also from Walmart inside of them – all given to me by rappers on the street of various cities all throughout the United States of America. We're talking D.C., we're talking Los Angeles, we're talking New Orleans. And actually, we're talking those three exact places today, because I will be live-reviewing three different mixtapes courtesy of rappers hailing from those locations. Let's get started. Okay, wait, I'm drunk, so I just decided that I'm going to do these while drunk lol.

DOT GIDDA

YouTube:
https://www.youtube.com/channel/UC04LmmWbxDk21crpb9GiI_g
Twitter:
https://twitter.com/darealdotg?lang=en
Spotify:
https://open.spotify.com/artist/6oIIuq4E9TmNHfn7qp5Zqn

Dot Gidda hails from Washington D.C. I bought his mixtape for exactly $3 on the street in front of a McDonald's directly after President Obama's second inauguration. Clearly a lot of things were happening and I decided that I would love to purchase this stranger's mixtape. It was my first mixtape ever and that's when I became addicted. Thank you, Dot Gidda. Anyway, let's get to reviewing.

MIXTAPE: THE REPRESENTATIVE

- Track 1: The Grind [Skit]
  Okay, so this is just a skit, so it's all right. He appears to be selling his own mixtape for $5 on the skit. Oh wait, it's over. Okay.

- Track 2: Me In My World
  The beat to this is pretty good. I wonder who produced it. Why don't we credit producers more? Anyway, I think he's talking about how he shouldn't apologize for being himself? Oh shit I'm already halfway done with the song – that was so fast. I really don't know what else to say about this other than he seems to be

living his own life and I am incredibly proud of him. Dot Gidda, if you're reading this I love you so much.

- Track 3: Stories Of A Lost Brother, Pt. 2
  Wait, where the fuck was part one? I feel so incomplete right now. How is he going to do me like this? Do I need his previous mixtape in order to understand this storyline? Man, he's smart. He seems to be apologizing to someone, I think? OMG, he ended it with saying, "Just wait until I get to part 3!" Wow……

- Track 4: Step Into The Bad Side
  Oh my god – this goes so hard! Y'all really need to listen to this right now. I wish y'all were with me. I don't know what he's saying, but the beat is really hard and he's rapping really fast. I do feel as if I am stepping into the bad side.

- Track 7: Somebody I Used To Know
  Oh shit, he did not spend any time making sure that I knew that this was a clear sample rap of Somebody That

I Used To Know by Gotye. I love this so much. He's rapping over the beat and the chorus. Amazing. Woah that song was so short. Damn.

- Track 11: Check Mail (Skit)
  How do I keep skipping so many songs? I am listening to them, but I just keep forgetting to write about them? Oops. Well, this is another skit. He's just playing voicemails that he's received. The first one is from some girl that he met at the club. The second one is from some guy who wants to collab with him. Oh, now it's over. Wow. I hope he's dating her and rapping with that guy.

RAHN G WIT IT

Facebook:
https://www.facebook.com/RahnG/
Twitter: https://twitter.com/rahng?lang=en
Spotify:
https://open.spotify.com/artist/0r6YzKaBMaiBAjvFBbku7L

Rahn G Wit It is one of the only rappers whose mixtape I bought but I never met. The story goes that I was walking the streets of Los Angeles one day, and I found a broken CD on the ground. I could still read the title of the disc and it happened to have Rahn G's social media information on it. I found him on Twitter and then told him about the situation. Rahn G graciously sent me a FREE mixtape in the mail. Thank you, Rahn G. Let's get to reviewing.

MIXTAPE: DOUBLE DOUBLE

- Track 1: Ball Hog
  Okay, damn. This guy has got bars and beats. I really dig this. It's not Kanye's Yeezus or anything, but it still goes pretty hard. I wish you could be listening to this with me right now. Is that something you would enjoy? Can we schedule this?

- Track 2: On The Grind ft. Me Eazie
  I wonder if the guy featured in this song is related to G-Eazy. Is that how rappers work? Similar to Drag Queens where you have a family and your names are sort of related in a way? I have to Google this. Okay, I could find literally nothing. Oh, the song is over now. I think it was good?

- Track 3: No Cups
  I just took a break to listen to the soundtrack to The Last Five Years, so this is gonna be confusing to my emotions. Anyway, this song is also pretty good. Damn, this is what I think of when I think of a mixtape. I'm gonna have to say that so far this is 10/10.

- Track 5: Party! ft. Me Eazie
  Sorry I'm too drunk to remember track 4. But this track is pretty good. The chorus is him repeating, "If I'mma die tomorrow, I'mma throw a party for tonight." Which is a good mindset honestly.

- Track 12: The Mission ft. Me Eazie
  Yet again, I am very sorry, but I'm going to skip the rest of the mixtape and go straight for the last song because I am too drunk for any of this right now. Why is Me Eazie in all of his songs? Are they like Macklemoore and Ryan Lewis together? Was this even a review?

SALT

Facebook:
https://www.facebook.com/DaRealSalt/
Google Play:
https://play.google.com/store/music/album/SALTYSALT_Da_Whole_Salt_Nothin_But_Da_Salt?id=B2ematsqzwdbodb25j7xswflaw

4
A Weird Interview:
http://www.music4breakfast.com/index.php/interview-with-salt/

Salt (or in some instances SaltySalt, for legal reasons probably) is a rapper from New Orleans. I was on Bourbon Street with a bunch of friends and he was asking everyone to buy his mixtape, as rappers do. I think I spent $10 on it, which is the most I've ever spent on a mixtape. Not only that, but I actually couldn't find the mixtape when looking for it, so I actually spent ten more dollars to buy it on Google Play, the only place I could find it online. I'm glad I'm investing so much in this specific individual. You're welcome, Salt. Let's get to reviewing.

MIXTAPE: DA WHOLE SALT & NOTHIN BUT DA SALT

- Track 2: Da Whole Salt
  DA WHOLE SAT & NOTHIN BUT DA SALT, BABY. That's what he says the entire song basically, but I'm not even mad. It's a pretty funny line and he says it SO seriously. I hope that women know all that salt is

not good for them. Also, this song is pretty good. It's more RnB than Rap / Hip-Hip, as the other ones were.

- Track 3: Salt Don't
  I've decided that I'm only going to review the songs that have the word 'Salt' in them, which is apparently TWELVE SONGS. This song actually reminds me of Luxurious by Gwen Stefani in a very weird way. I guess you'll just have to listen to it yourself. Buy it on Google Play because that's the only place I could find it.

- Track 4: All Salted Out
  Oh, now we're getting funky! I really love how he sings and then he's his own hype-man in the background. What exactly does "All Salted Out" mean? He keeps saying it and then referring to overcoming a loss. But, like, I still don't understand the idiom I assume he just made up for his brand.

- Track 6: Asalt
  Now, this one's a pun! I wonder if

he's the kind of person who goes to late-night diners with people and decides to tell jokes about salt and pepper opposed to having meaningful conversations. Okay, wait the song has started and I can confirm that he is this kind of person. That's all I have to say about this track.

- Track 7: Salt Shakers
  "I don't understand these salt shakers." After listening to the first line in this song, it's clear that he calls his haters "salt shakers." Which is great because most artists in music nowadays have a pet name for their fan base, but he only has one for his haters.

- Track 8: Salt In Da Game
  I wonder how many times he says "salt" total in this mixtape. I really want to count, but then I'd have really no one to share it with because no one has ever heard of him and my friends definitely won't care.

- Track 10: Salt Reign

- Track 11: Salt Twist
  This song is great and important commentary about women and their appreciation for Salt. Now he's just naming a ton of cities off, but I really don't think it's for a tour or anything.

- Track 12: Salts Got Da Flava
  Throughout this mixtape, he keeps referring to Salt as a seasoning and flavor. Which, I guess may be true? I'm really not about to Google the specifics of salt.

- Track 13: Salt's Way
  This legit started out sounding like a High School Musical track. I respect that. This entire song is about how he feels like he needs to have the final say in any relationship he's in. That's a bit unhealthy, but maybe it's someone's kink to be bossed around? In that situation, this song is very good for that one person.

- Track 15: Shakem Up Salt
  Can y'all believe how many songs this mixtape has? And how almost all of them refer to his name / the

"seasoning." I wonder how many of these CDs he's sold. And how many times he's had to explain his rap name.

- Track 19: Salt Lick
  I love a good salt lick. I don't know what else to say about this song – that's really the only review I have. I love the title. Thank you, mister Salt.

Please support the arts, especially the ones that come from the street and are from people who rap.

REAL ENTERTAINMENT™

Have you ever been watching a show and thought, "I really want to insert myself into this writing process and send ideas to the creators of this show even though no one has asked me to?" So have I. And lucky for you, I'm going to tell you about real shows that I watch and the ideas that I've come up with that I think are better than the actual content on said show. Then, I'm going to do some of my own inserting into YOUR life – I'm going to make up some shows completely on the spot and give you complete freedom to create them. This is a service I like to call Real Entertainment™. I take shows that truly need a lot of help, and I write to the creators to help them make said shows better. Likewise, I give you ideas to create successful shows! I know my own genius is diminished because of this, but it's okay because I'm a martyr and live for you: my fans. Boy, I sure hope people who work in television are reading this right now!

    Have you ever heard of Black Mirror, created by Charlie Brooker? So, it's basically this technological-dystopian show from the UK completely written by Brooker. He has stated, "[The episodes] are all about the way we live now – and the way we might be living in 10 minutes' time if we're clumsy." Basically, it shows how our technology – YouTube, Rating Systems, AI, etc. – could turn on us in such a short amount of time, and how, because of that, we may be already living in a dystopian society. Interesting, huh? This show has gained wide popularity over the years, and has even been incredibly hard for people to watch. So, I'm gonna create a list of my own Black Mirror episode ideas and describe them as best as I can! Why do I think I'm more fit to do this than Charlie Brooker himself? Well, maybe because my ideas are actually relatable! Here we go!

BLACK MIRROR EPISODE IDEAS

- ***Fit In With Fitbit***
  So basically it'll be placed in a universe in which everyone is totally obsessed with walking 10,000 steps each day. And, like, business people / governments have totally monetized walking. In order to get your steps in, you need to pay an hourly amount to activate your legs. Or something. Idk, I'm sure Charlie could make it work.

- ***Driverless Planes***
  We've all heard of driverless cars, right? Well in this universe, planes are the next vehicles to boot their own pilots. You get on a plane and no one is there to offer you a cookie or a small cup of ginger ale. You get really thirsty and hungry throughout the flight, but no one cares because the plane is the only attendant you need during your flight to Paris. And, like, somehow there's even less legroom in front of you.

- ***"Hey, Google."***
  In this universe, you can say "Hey, Google" at any time and a virtual woman will pop

up next to you. Only, every time you ask her something, she doesn't understand you. If you say, "Will you tell me the height of that building in feet?," she'll probably say, "Sorry – I didn't get that. Did you want me to look up Chinese food nearby?" And it'll be a total inconvenience, if anything. Scary.

- ***Disconnected***
  This takes place in a universe in which your Bluetooth is, like, constantly disconnecting. Like, all the time. And it sucks. No one's happy.

And there you have it: my ideas about how Charlie Brooker can start making his Black Mirror show much better. Luckily for him, this one-time service of Real Entertainment™ is free. You're welcome, Charlie.

Okay, on to the next television content creator who I think could use my help: Nathan Fielder. Nathan Fielder is a Canadian-born, Los Angeles-based comedian who has a comedy show on Comedy Central called "Nathan For You." Anyone who has seen the show knows that a business degree is no longer relevant in order to create and implement amazing ideas to help small businesses flourish. That's what Fielder proves in this show as he goes to dozens of businesses all over the Los Angeles area and helps them market their products and services in unusual, and often cringe-y, ways. Well, Mr. Fielder, I have some ideas of my own, and they are also free to you thanks to my very successful business: Real Entertainment™.

NATHAN FOR YOU EPISODE IDEAS

- ***The Anne Frank House Game***
  The Anne Frank House is a historic home-turned-museum building that remembers the Jewish diarist Anne Frank, who died during the Holocaust. She hid in the attic of a house with her family and had to be very quiet so that the Nazi soldiers wouldn't find

them. The Anne Frank House is visited by over a million people each year. But wouldn't that number be higher if a game was involved? For double the price of entering the house, people could stuff themselves in the attic of the house with a bunch of strangers while a couple museum employees dressed in appropriate Nazi uniform walk around downstairs asking, "Are you hiding any Jews?" A noise decibel device could be placed on the wall in the attic, and if people raise the noise in the room higher than a certain decibel, they lose.

- **'Whites Only' Bread Shop**
  Bread has been around for thousands of years, and it was only a matter of time before people began to realize that they could utilize capitalism to sell this dough to earn dough! However, bread shops are becoming less and less popular as people realize that other food is so much better. What bread shop owners don't realize is that their shop is also unpopular because they're making all the wrong kinds of bread. We all know the majority of people prefer white bread. So why not give into popular demand and institute a 'Whites Only' policy? If these business people would only sell white bread, surely

their sales and customer base would only increase. Likewise, changing the name of a bread shop to 'Whites Only Bread Shop' could indicate to the public that you are selling what they truly want.

- **Naughty Emoji Chain Text Service**
  Business is tough! Texting isn't! We've all seen struggling businesses, but we've also received a sexed-up chain text filled to the brim with emojis. Wouldn't it make sense to put these two things together? If businesses were to send out naughty emoji chain texts, their products would immediately become desirable and people would flock to their doorstep. But creating these chain texts isn't easy – it takes literally hours to craft the perfect one. So why not create a service to help businesses market their products in a new and desirable fashion? Entirely staffed by teenagers with iPhones, the 'Naughty Emoji Chain Text' Service could bring a business's financial status from bankrupt to banking!

Don't you think these ideas are foolproof? In fact, remember the naughty emoji chain text from chapter three? Well, that is a very good example of how businesses could utilize this service in order to increase their customer base. Old people are dying and millenials are rising! Anyway, I hope Nathan sees these episode ideas and decides to implement them into his show. I'm really glad I can be helping these struggling artists come up with better ideas. And for the low cost of nothing! That's the true beauty of Real Entertainment™.

Okay, now for the moment that you have been waiting for: where I give you content and you are free to create.

Well, what if we went off of something that has already been written – like that whole Anne Frank shit I wrote. That was pretty problematic, right? What if there was a show centered entirely around problematic content? Except the twist? It's a meta television show presented as a game show to the public and as a network start-up / focus group documentary to the contestants. Sounds really dumb – so we're on the right track. Basically, twelve to fifteen people are going to be coerced inside a room under the understanding that they are to be the focus group for a series of shows that are trying to make it onto a new television network. The "network" tells them that they are on a documentary about the process of creating a network and utilizing focus groups. That's why they aren't weirded out when there are cameras on them. Anyway, they get shown trailers to television shows such as the Anne Frank House Game, to which we time how long it takes someone in the room to say something along the lines of, "Isn't this problematic?" The entire show is basically a game show to the public that attempts to understand how long it takes the average human being to stand-up for what they believe in and say, "What the fuck?"

    Another show idea: People Who Used To Be Scene, Where Are They Now?

    This next television show idea is a sugar daddy reality television show that is sort of like The Voice in the fact that there are four sugar daddies deciding which women they want to shower in money, sort of like Big Brother in the fact that there are 12 women who live together in isolation for a full year while competing to win a sugar daddy, and sort of like The Bachelor in that this entire show idea is really dumb. So, the entire time these women are creating general havoc and drama in the house for the public to enjoy, the sugar daddies are watching them and deciding the pros and cons of each woman. However, the meta plot twist is that these four sugar daddies are unknowingly competing to be the top sugar daddy who will get to shower the winning woman in money. The women and the public vote one woman out each month, and the final woman standing will win the opportunity to go on a date with the last sugar daddy standing. But here's the part where the show turns into NEXT, basically: the woman has never seen the sugar daddies before. Therefore, when the final sugar daddy and the final woman meet for the first time, she has the opportunity to scream, "THAT'S THAT ON THAT" and end the entire date, effectively rendering the entire year-long television show pointless.

On to the next one. A documentary about a Flashmob Curator. Except no one watches it.

Anyway, those are all of the ideas I have for you, reader. I guess if you want to think of your own television show ideas: good luck. Just copy something that's already on the air and make it more ridiculous – that seems to be the go-to formula nowadays.

And that's what I've always loved about television.

Thank you for tuning into Real Entertainment™.

NOW THAT YOU'VE TRAVERSED MY MIND AND LIFE EXPERIENCES, DO YOU WANT MY ADVICE?

I'm not really qualified to give anyone advice on any level whatsoever, but I'll go ahead and tell you some of the life lessons that I have learned on this journey.

1. Live in a city that borders on two different time zones. Imagine that. If you did that, it means you could eat at your favorite restaurant AND THEN hop over to the earlier time zone and eat again even though the later time zone's restaurant is CLOSED for the day. Talk about

cheating the construct of time and capitalism.

2. Don't buy a yearlong gym membership from your friend Jared. Actually, just don't go to the gym at all. The next thing you know, it's been a year and you didn't step foot in the gym once, even though it was right next door to your apartment complex. You'll find yourself questioning why you decided that "Donate To A Gym" was a good bucket list entry.

3. You know that irrational fear of cars passing you by because the driver might shoot you? The one you've had since you were a small child? I don't have any advice for that.

4. Be okay with people accidentally misgendering you at the Whataburger drive-thru – it's inevitable.

5. If you're ever sad, just read the IMDb reviews for the 2007 Disney Channel Original Movie Jump In! starring

Corbin Bleu and Keke Palmer. I've included a couple entries below:

Good movie
Author: L HH from Vietnam
14 June 2011

To be honest, my dad was going to work when he accidentally saw the movie on TV. And he was almost late for work because of it.

Surprisingly good
Author: mercywriter from United States
20 February 2007

*** This review may contain spoilers ***

No major spoilers in this, but I want to be safe.

What a delightful surprise. My kids wanted to see this, and when it came on the Disney channel we all watched. I had a book in my lap, figuring I wouldn't find the movie all that interesting. But the book stayed closed in my lap (except for during commercials.) A nice movie. Clean. A message of "violence doesn't get you anywhere." And many more. It even taught some nice family values. In one scene, the boy says some harsh things to his father, but as soon as he sees the hurt in his father's eyes, he says he's sorry. A nice and rare example in this day and age of movies. All in all, a good family movie. I recommend it. Oh yeah, and the Double Dutch scenes are pretty good, too. :)

One of the worst films I have ever seen...ever
Author: Mostafa Rachwani from Australia
3 January 2009

This is a disgusting piece of garbage. Simple as that. The acting is horrifyingly wooden, the direction is woeful and the script? I just wanted to kill myself every time the characters opened their mouthes. The situations were amazingly UN-realistic, I mean how many people seriously go to a skip rope competition? And why is everyone such a stereotype? Who seriously even would laugh at that, or tease someone because of that? Are these teenagers or 5 year olds? It was just a supremely irritating film, and highly advise anyone with half a brain cell to avoid this at all costs.

jump out!

Author: lobo_plawecki

2 June 2007

6. Do you remember when Chick-Fil-A got #ExPoSeD for being, like, anti-gay or something? And then all of the gay people got pissed and decided that the logical thing to do was to kiss each other on a very specific day in front of every single Chick-Fil-A in the nation? Well, like, that not only created great marketing for Chick-Fil-

A, for one, but also it created this weird love event where everyone was macking on each other at this fast food establishment. What I mean is: after the whole gay kissing happened, the STRAIGHT people then decided that they'd have their own day to kiss each other in front of Chick-Fil-As around the nation. What is up with people??? Regardless, what Chick-Fil-A's real crime was is the fact that they got, like, everyone in the entire USofA to make out with each other in front of their establishments. And since then, I've been eating there.

7. Was that last point even advice?

Okay, that's all the advice I have to give! That was actually better than I expected.

AFTERWORD

I just wrote a BOOK! Fuck you, mom! Now I'm going to drive to Chili's and eat all of their food. See ya later!

ABOUT THE AUTHOR

Ashley Jane Richardson is a human being that resides in Los Angeles, California.

www.ingramcontent.com/pod-product-compliance
Lightning Source LLC
Chambersburg PA
CBHW061647040426
42446CB00010B/1622